Pedro Eloy

BUY-ME!

Swaying minds and influencing behaviours
through mainstream advertising

For further publications or to contact the author visit:
www.NewMediaForBusiness.com

ISBN-13: 978-1463572921
ISBN-10: 1463572921

Design by Cristina Lopo

"Good communication is as stimulating
as black coffee, and just as hard to sleep after."

Anne Morrow Lindbergh

Table of Contents

Chapter 17

FOREWORD

By Fernando Santos
Managing Director, OasisEurope

With the book *Buy-Me! Swaying minds and influencing behaviours through mainstream advertising,* Pedro Eloy illustrates the main consumption trends and tendencies at the turn of the 20th Century, in a clear, concise and objective manner. With a simple, straightforward and easy-to-follow writing, Pedro lays out the main challenges and hurdles felt by both companies wishing to launch, reposition, reactivate or simply sell their brands and products in the marketplace, and advertising & communication agencies wishing to promote them, via the design, implementation and execution of adequate and efficient campaigns.

By using real-life examples and taking from the works of reputed authors, Pedro Eloy successfully frames and supports his opinions and points of view, providing a global perspective and unique insight on the consumer behaviour to advertising messages, consumption habits and communication trends, whilst taking us by the hand and leading the reader into a nostalgic journey trough the eighties and the nineties, allowing the reminiscence of the adverts that have subtly, but undoubtedly shaped our childhood.

.....

Fernando Santos is the Managing Director of OasisEurope, an international Management Consulting company focusing on retail management with offices in Portugal and Poland. He was owner and CEO of Z-Publicidade, an innovative and out-of-the-box advertising agency which revolutionized the Portuguese communication scenario, having received several national and international prizes and having been the first advertising agency in Portugal to be awarded a Gold Lion at the Cannes Advertising Festival in the year 2000.

Fernando Santos has been responsible for promoting, developing the strategic framework, conceptual planning and execution of campaigns for Mercedes-Benz, Red Bull, Feira Nova and Sara Lee.

PREFACE

During the eighties and nineties Portugal went through a period of dramatic changes across almost every sector of its social and economic framework, which resulted in a change of both mindset and behaviours of agents, influencers and players operating in the different sectors and industries. At the same time, a new paradigm emerged from within the Portuguese society, both in terms of lifestyle as well as in what concerns patterns and trends in consumption and consumer behaviour.

The European Community accession in 1986, followed by a period of political and economical stability during the XI e XII *Governos Constitucionais* lead by Prime Minister Cavaco Silva (1987-1995), enabled Portugal to enact and implement a series of structural reforms which resulted in the establishment of a truly social Market Economy; by introducing fiscal, labour and social reforms, Portugal created the necessary conditions to allow the entrance of the Private Sector in the most important strategic sectors of its growing economy. The liberalization of the media, gave rise to the emergence of privately-held radio and television operators, the modernization of national infrastructures and access routes, within borders and to neighbouring countries, allowed for greater proximity with national and European decision centres, conferring mobility to national and international agents and facilitating the movement of goods and services; the entrance of foreign capital, either trough external investment or via the reform and revival of the Portuguese financial sector, gave rise to multivalent partnerships, which encouraged the establishment of large multinationals in Portuguese soil and reinforced the country's strategic cooperation with foreign entities.

In terms of consumption patterns, the opening of the Portuguese market to external agents made available a series of goods and services that were only known to a small percentage of its population, with superior education and higher available income, able to travel abroad and knowledgeable of the latest trends in fashion, electric apparels, decoration items and fast moving consumer goods, such as food products. At the same time, and in order to respond to the growing demand, the Portuguese retail sector went through a remarkable restructuring process; the first *hipermercados*, large retail chains and department stores, made their appearance and began to rapidly expand across the country, in a concerted effort to better respond to the rising and growing needs and requirements of Portuguese consumers, which demanded new products and product categories, traditionally not represented within the portfolios of the major distributors.

The increase in available income, together with the expansion of the product and service portfolio fuelled a radical change in the attitudes and behaviours of Portuguese consumers, which became more informed, and consequently more challenging and demanding.

In order for companies to sell their goods and services, it no longer sufficed to have products placed on the market; instead, considerable efforts needed to be developed in order to create the need inside the consumer's mind, then trigger the will and motivation to buy and finally to convince the buyer to go to the store and make the purchase.

Influencing consumers and their predisposition to purchase was no longer an easy task- advertising agencies soon realized that the mere adjustment of foreign communication campaigns, developed for countries with different cultures and lifestyles and subsequently dubbed in Portuguese was simply insufficient. As a result, advertising started to be designed and produced with the Portuguese consumer mindset at heart. Newly innovative pieces became mandatory, often disruptive and considerably bold, but also conciliatory and traditional; however different or similar, all were created to be profoundly coherent with the assigned target and strategically aligned with their social, economical and cultural background.

The appearance of small, out-of-the-box and immensely creative agencies fully prepared and capable to respond to these new emerging trends was one of the consequences of the profound changes seen by the communication industry . In fact, the entire sector suffered an enormous revolution driven by the need to respond efficiently and effectively to the redefinition and restructuring of consumption patterns and habits. The choice of an agency became a determinant factor in the emerging Portuguese consumption paradigm. Its versatility, its track record, its resources – human, operational and networking wise – were carefully assessed and evaluated by potential clients, companies wishing to perform sales, before deciding to sign-up with an agency to successfully promote their respective goods and services. With all these new developments, errors have also been made, some of which fatal to both the client and to the advertising agency.

This book summarizes the main trends in advertising and communication at the end of the nineties, addressing consumers' attitudes, reactions and behaviours as well as the main challenges and most important the changes felt by the advertising and communication agencies whilst developing promotional campaigns. Throughout the text, and in order to better illustrate and support the opinions and conclusions expressed therein, real life examples of strategies, campaigns, events and facts that have been implemented, executed and observed are used, as means to probing and rattling the reader's brain with memories that will allow a better framing of the issues addressed in this book, allowing the reader to take from its own experience and draw its own conclusions. The text also draws from reputed authors' points of view and opinions, to convey the most consensual – or the most extreme - underlying thoughts and ideas at the time, allowing the reader to become fully immersed in the enormously creative, radically dynamic and immensely challenging atmosphere that was a characteristic of the times depicted in the present book.

....

Pedro Eloy is a specialist in the development and implementation of New Media & online strategies, working with top management and entrepreneurs in both local and multinational companies in the design and implementation of integrated e-solutions addressing the launch, growth and sustainability of products & brands , the development and expansion of the overall business and the search and establishment of novel products.

Experienced in a variety of industries such as retail, banking & finance, advertising, non-profit and entertainment, Pedro Eloy has selected, trained and lead multidisciplinary teams on the conception, planning and execution of a multitude of New Media, online and IT projects.

Whilst in Portugal, Pedro Eloy was responsible for the Communications Department of Infordesporto, a pioneer company centred in delivering integrated television and e-based solutions for the sports industry and consulted for TVLab, the organization responsible for the local implementation and rollout of the Interactive Television Project, in collaboration with Microsoft.

In the USA, Pedro joined Turner Network Television, TNTLA, taking in hands the development and implementation of online marketing programs and promotional campaigns for prestigious ceremonies of the Hollywood film industry.

In the UK, Pedro Eloy worked with the ICC Research Foundation to support their online strategy and the implementation of related e-projects and with GH Solutions in the rollout of their global marketing & sales strategy, including the management of its *Global Partner & Reseller Network*. Pedro Eloy has also worked closely with the Paris-based International Chambers of Commerce (ICC) in the development and implementation of online & New Media solutions.

Within the Social Responsibility sector, Pedro has colaborated with both Toronto-based Caritas (Canada) and Lisbon-based NPVSocial (Portugal) in the design and execution of e-based solutions.

Pedro Eloy has lived and worked in Portugal, Canada, USA, the UK and Hong Kong where he is currently the Director of New Media & IT for the Fung Global Institute.

CHAPTER 1

INFORMATION & SOCIETY

In 1950, the Greek word '*Megametropolis*' (or megacities) could only be used to describe two cities in the world, London and New York, the only two in the world with over eight million dwellers. The growth of worldwide economies, fuelled by a production boost that followed the post-WWII period, brought forth new and more prosperous lifestyles, which in turn, fuelled birth rates across the globe, especially throughout Europe and North America, enabling and allowing companies to start working on sales and promotional strategies that went beyond local, regional and national borders.

The surge of large multinational corporations fostered the migration of families in search of employment opportunities, resulting in the emergence of newly populated cities, growing in numbers and in population, bustling with new blood and available income to spend. The rise in demand was both cause and consequence of a rise in the offering, and companies sought innovative solutions to allow the restructure of their supply chains and productive structures - with a resulting decrease in costs and increase in revenues - as well as a redesign of their sourcing strategies, which progressively turned from local to global solutions, driving the growth and expansion of more distant and traditionally underdeveloped economies that slowly started to become important players as cost-quality efficient suppliers. The search for business partners willing and able to respond to the demands of the Western developed open-market economies gave rise to a series of social, economical, political and structural reforms across the world, opening up a series of unparalleled and exciting opportunities to those willing to recognise and take advantage of these upcoming opportunities.

The lift of economic and commercial restrictions towards the import and export of goods & services to and from former Iron Curtain countries, together with the loss of political and economical dominance of the former USSR and its subsequent demise as a unified republic of member states, promoted a new world order, with recently independent nations, possessing a highly qualified labour force and avidly claiming for employment.

The increase in job opportunities within these

emerging countries, mainly driven by the pull from western economies in search for low-cost labour, resulted in a profound restructuring of local societies, which benefitted from an increase in their economic status, followed by a growth in birth rates, especially across Eastern Europe and Asia. Nowadays, the number of Megametropolis across the world is much higher than that observed in 1950, with experts forecasting that, around 2015, there will be 33 Megametropolis, where 19 will be located in Asia.

Current Megametropolis simply cannot be referred to as common 'cities', as their underlying pillars are much broader and wider than common cities. In truth, Megametropolis are living, breathing urban conglomerates, with evermore expanding borders. Rich or poor, young or old, these cities of excess face common pains and suffer similar ailments, such as housing deficiencies, pollution, over-population, insecurity, social inequalities and exclusion. At the same time, they are avid and eager consumers of products, mostly supplied by multinational companies.

The opening of new markets combined with the rise of untapped segments and potential targets allowed companies to expand their portfolios and diversify their business, focusing on new trends and opportunities. The globalization of local economies became a commonly used expression and, what more, a true reality, in which national structures and decision centres are loosing in both influence and importance. The emergence of new technologies, together with the massification of internet-connected computers and the use of innovative, efficient and low-cost communication solutions contributed to shorten the distance between individuals, companies and even countries, enhancing the flow of information at a global scale and transforming individual scocieties in global information societies, in which *all* is known, *all* is communicated and *all* is shared. This knowledge paradigm gave birth to a new generation of consumers, highly specialized and infinitely informed, where the decisions to purchase and consume are thought beforehand and diligently compared at both local and global scales.

Together with social and economic development, the free flow of information and technological breakthrough pioneered and fuelled remarkable scientific discoveries in a multitude of areas, allowing for an improvement in the quality of life, as well as an increase in the overall life expectancy, giving rise to a growing and extremely exciting new segment of consumers with available income and, most importantly, time to spend it. Some marketers refer to this segment as the 'Silver Surfers', grey-haired, mature men and women over 60s willing and able to cruise through the remainder of their lives enjoying it to the most and fully savouring ever moment. Others simply refer to it as the *elderly*, often referring to special demands this group requires, such as social, medical, intellectual or even physical needs. Young in body, in mind, in both, or simply at heart, the fact is that this segment has increased in numbers in almost every developed economy, leading companies to rethink and reformulate their offering in order to better address and fully serve this segment.

CHAPTER 2

THE ACT OF PURCHASING

Consumers question everything, from prices, to conditions, to warranties. That is an established truth. They are sensitive to a brand's value and reputation, they are becoming hardened negotiators in pursuit of more favourable terms of business, they research, analyze and come to the conclusion of what to buy, where to buy, when to buy, how much to buy, and, finally, whether to buy a second time or not; they look for the product offerings with the most added value; they are informed individuals living in a world that offers numerous options and substitutes. Nowadays, more than ever, consumers demand to be given value for their money.

The concept of Value is a three-fold combination of – apparently independent – variables: quality, service and price. Quality, usually referred to by the letter Q, represents the tangible characteristics, or attributes, of the products, which may be easily measured by using appropriate industry standards. For instance, the quality of a simple white T-shirt is measured by the fabric and threads from which it is made of – type of material, weight, homogeneity in density and colour, resilience... – as well as from the excellence in craftsmanship, upon cutting the fabric, sowing in all the seams and delivering a fine, well-finished, tailored garment. Service, usually referred to by the letter S, corresponds to both the available ancillary services associated to a certain product as well as to their respective perceived value, or utility level, as seen from the customer's perspective. Price, usually referred to by the letter P, concerns the actual monetary amount paid by the customer to acquire the product. These three variables combined are both necessary and sufficient to fully describe the value proposition presented to the customer.

Quality, by itself, although necessary, is no longer sufficient; an excellent customer service level, although much desired and sought for, will not be fully satisfactory unless associated with other product characteristics and/or benefits, even if intangible. Finally the pricing, even if greatly reduced, will not ensure long term sales growth and its sustainability. Only when combined, will the three variables Q, S and P become an appealing and attractive value proposition that may meet or exceed the customer's expectations and, ultimately, result in an effective act of purchase.

The key is to understand how the customer perceives and ranks the value of a product, and then act on this understanding to develop both efficient and effective communication and selling strategies. Perceived value explains phenomena such as why, in certain segments or categories, companies offering the most expensive brands and products hold the largest market shares; consumers' price sensitivity to a product or a certain category of products will be evermore reduced whenever the perceived value is evermore increased. An example of this is found in the automobile industry: the Volkswagen group manufactures cars under a variety of brands, from the inexpensive Skoda to the young and dynamic Seat, from the wide-ranged Volkswagen, to the high-end executive Audi, all sharing similar, if not identical engines, platforms, manufacturing procedures and quality systems, but with price ranges set according to their different positioning strategies.

Customers will feel happy to face higher prices and buy an Audi, which will give them status, and position in society – and will make them look good when driving by their neighbours – than acquire a souped-up Skoda, even if with a more potent engine, a finer binary and a more efficient weight-to-power relation. It also explains why many companies, involved in constant price wars may end up bankrupt.

The consumer, more informed and therefore more difficult to be influenced or persuaded to buy a certain product, has fully adjusted to the new purchasing trends; however, the levels of infidelity - in other words, the possibility for a consumer to trade a certain brand or product for competitive substitute -has also become a regular practice, with companies developing efforts to encourage brand loyalty and customer retention, in order to sustain ongoing sales.

During the nineties, in Portugal, customer infidelity had reached levels surpassing 30%, which is considered, by specialists, to be very high. The Portuguese consumer could, therefore, be labelled a chameleon-type consumer, not loyal to a specific brand or product, enacting the choice only upon acquiring the item and resorting to substitutes for either rational or irrational motives, or a combination of both, or even simply for the fact that, at the time, a more attractive alternative was being made available.

As an example of a rational motive for being unfaithful to a brand or product, consider the case of a business executive, who will travel first class whenever flying on business – the airfare being paid by the company – but who will purchase economy seats whenever taking his family on vacation – the airfare, in latter case, being paid for by his own money. Another example of being unfaithful to a brand is the emotional setting: take a young girl who will switch from one perfume to another, depending on the outfit she wears, or on the boy she is dating. Finally, regarding the existence of more attractive alternatives, think of the housewife who will often switch from one floor cleaning detergent to another, depending on which is in promotion, whenever she goes to the supermarket.

To foster and successfully maintain high customer loyalty rates, there are several techniques, methodologies and programmes usually employed by companies aiming at promoting a closer and more intimate relationship between the customer, the brand or product and the manufacturing/distributing company. Studies have shown that recruiting new customers is usually three to five times more expensive than maintaining and cultivating the already existing ones. To increase customer loyalty, it is absolutely necessary to investigate and identify the main causes that drive customer insatisfaction, especially those that lead them to either refrain from acquiring a certain product or service or the causes for seeking a competitor offering.

An experienced consumer will not hesitate to switch from brand to brand, from product to product, depending on the value proposition. He/she will prefer larger stores, such as hypermarkets (big supermarket stores) or large department stores, which not only offer their own brands at lower prices and with similar quality parameters, but also often dictate their own terms and conditions to producers and manufacturers, in an attempt to maintain a control on price, portfolio and availability. Such procedures reinforce the asymmetries in the choice of products, stores and purchasing experiences, consequently contributing to a decrease in loyalty and retention rates.

So that a purchase can happen, the customer needs to know that a specific product / service exist and that it is available for purchasing (awareness). The available offering has to be associated with a set of benefits – be them real or perceived – valued by the customer and meeting the customer's existing or newly created needs (positioning). Finally, the product or service will need to be placed in a high level of the customer's hierarchy of preferences, so that, whenever the need associated to the product or service comes to mind, the product or service, so intimately associated with the need, will immediately be remembered (recall). The customer must then need to be encouraged to acquire the product or service (promotion).

After becoming convinced that competitors' offerings (substitutes) will neither fully satisfy the intrinsic needs nor provide the same benefits, the customer must find the products and services easily available, either at a nearby store or online, and priced at a level that agrees with the customer's willingness to disburse the required amount (share of wallet). Finally, after the purchase has occurred, the customer needs to feel some sort of satisfaction or gratification for having acquired the product or service, and one that will match – or, ideally, exceed - the customer's initial expectations.

In summary, the purchasing process is a complex one, comprising several stages, at both emotional and logic levels, and triggered by diverse and distinct stimuli. Starting with the onset of the need, it is followed by the rationalization of the need/problem definition and then by the search for available information, allowing for a decision to be made, then a purchase and a subsequent evaluation, which will provide feedback that enables the customer to choose between repeating the purchase or switching brands.

The act of purchasing motivated by the product's characteristics as well as by other tangible and rational motives (real benefits) is also very much influenced by emotional, intangible, image-related or perception benefits. The promotional campaign set in place to prompt the sale needs to be carefully adjusted in order to succeed. As an example, the purchase of a perfume is a purely subjective decision -when selling a perfume one is never told that it will serve simply to mask one's smelly and sometimes unpleasant bodily odours, but rather that the perfume will transport its user to a sensuous and luscious scenario, populated by movie stars and sports champions and young, vibrant, stylish, hip characters.

A campaign aiming at promoting a perfume will have to, therefore appeal to emotional concepts drawing to and recalling beauty, attitude, lifestyle, self-esteem and purchasing power - in summary, to intangible values, since the perceive benefits of the product in question greatly outweigh the real benefits it offers. On the other hand, the purchase of an industrial welding machine is a purely objective decision, and its acquisition will obey rigorous specification parameters, such as power, output capacity, size, robustness, energy consumption, durability, delivery times and maintenance costs. In this case, the real benefit – the ability to weld with the highest yield possible at the smaller costs possible - is the determining factor.

For most consumption goods, shopping is an action that corresponds less to the satisfaction of real needs – albeit that being an obvious underlying motive – than it is becoming a moment of pure entertainment. Nowadays, the simple act of buying an environmentfriendly, low consumption, 100W lamp is more than just picking the one with the right fitting and power off the shelf to lit up one's living room; it is really a sensory adventure, subtly coloured in light pink, evanescent green or withering pale-blue, with light strokes of purple and lavender, to calm your mood and relax your body, while, at the same time, preserving Planet Earth for future generations – ones' children, grandchildren, great-grandchildren and respective spawn. This appeal to intangible qualities, evermore present in promotional campaigns is also being transported to the points of sale (POS), as a means to attract customers and lure them into making a purchase.

"Frame" magazine depicts in its August 1999 issue, through a variety of examples, how specific branded stores such as GAP and Nike, as well as entire shopping malls, are becoming entertainment destinations, where the act of buying is only a small portion of the full store experience.

Current trends indicate that the customer is willing to pay not only for the purchased product, but also for the overall shopping adventure, which allows POS to charge accordingly. As such, designing and building commercial spaces has become a very sensible issue – with an importance comparable to that of the actual products or services sold within - with architects, engineers and brand experts working together to provide consumers an overall integrated experience, alluring them inside, where they can sample the variety of product and service offerings, whilst being entertained by the surrounding environment.

Accortding to Charles Handy, business management expert, the last few years have brought forth an extremely materialistic era, in which the main objective is focused on the demand for goods in quantities that go beyond what is considered to be strictly necessary.

Many of us, especially the younger generations, have grown up in the illusion that concepts, such as war or famine, simply do not exist or cannot affect us, while firmly believing in the inexhaustible supply of products and the lack of limits to its availability. As such, our generation exhibits growing anxiety pains, leading to the continuous demand of not only new and improved products & services but also of something that goes beyond the pure act of consumption, by itself no longer fully satisfactory.

Emotion, or better, the search for emotions tied to the act of purchase, has therefore become the solution - in the words of Adam Smith, "the endless search for useless things". Useless or not, the fact is that consumers will buy these goods because they feel motivated to do so. In fact, for every real, objective, tangible and specific need, it is possible to enumerate a series of individual, subjective, intangible needs, which, although unrelated to the product itself - its features or intrinsic characteristics - will act as consumption drivers:

Playing a certain role in society: Many activities are acquired behaviours, traditionally expected and accepted by societies as being an integral part of a certain position or role – mother, housewife, husband, student, businessman… Individuals easily accept these behaviours as a pre-requirement to the role they fulfil, or feel compelled to fulfil, and act upon them by enacting and participating in what can be labelled as 'expected activities'. As an example, a housewife is expected to go shopping at the supermarket during the day, at 'business hours', preferably during the morning, when fresher fruits and vegetables are usually found. She will also visit several stores to get the right products at the right prices, often taking advantage of current promotions; a businesswoman will only get to the supermarket after a day's work and will prefer to visit one single store, even if paying a higher price for the products she acquires.

Entertainment: Going shopping can become an entertainment opportunity, a break from daily routine. It may also be turned into a "free" family experience, without any need for advanced planning or preparation. Looking at the masses of people that wander – apparently - aimlessly through the corridors of large, colourful, appellative shopping malls reinforces the belief that shopping can be a hobby, and a delightful one! Stores take advantage of this by promoting ancillary events, such as exhibitions and shows, by creating periodic 'themes' according to which decorations, music, lights and sometimes even smells are brought out to add to the look-and-feel experience. Stores attract visitors to their midst, offering a fully-flavoured entertainment setting that will encourage consumption.

Self-gratification: Different emotional states will bear different weights upon the motives that lead to shopping. A person may enter a store simply because he or she feels bored at the moment – and actually buy something – or may go to the mall simply because he/she is feeling lonely and earning to see other people. The same person may go deliberately to a certain store to buy something for him/herself, something that can only be found there, or to look for something to offer a significant other. Studies have shown that shopping can also be very efficient against feelings of anxiety and depression.

The simple act of making a purchase can act as an emotional trigger, impacting on self-awareness and reinforcing self-esteem, with subjects finding shopping as an alternative to pharmaceuticals. In such cases, the act of purchasing is not motivated by the expected utility of consumption, but by the emotinonal and social process of shopping.

Keeping up with the latest trends: Products are intimately related to one's daily activities; they are symbols that reflect attitudes and lifestyles. Many people, usually referred to as early adopters, are interested in keeping up to date with what concerns the latest fashion trends, the latest innovations in telecommunications, the latest releases in IT-related gadgets. Although this learning process may take place with or without the need for an actual purchase being made, the fact remains that these early adopters are more willing to purchase novelties.

Physical activity: An urban environment, characterized by diversified and accessible transportation means, private or collective, allied to an intense and, sometimes, regretfully less than ideal work-life balance does not leave much room for people to engage in outdoor activities or regular exercise programmes.

Shopping can provide a way to exercise both mind and body; walking in and out of stores at a mall, or perusing a variety of stores at the busiest shopping districts are viewed by customers as pleasurable activities, preferred by many as cheaper and more fulfilling than year-round memberships at the local gyms.

Sensorial Stimuli: Stores offer customers endless sensorial stimuli. When strolling around the corridors, customers are given the opportunity of admiring, touching and actually trying the store's latest products, whilst observing other customers, their preferences, behaviours and demeanours. They find pleasure in perceiving the products as their own, even if for just a brief moment, they become excited upon contemplating the possibility of taking the products home with them, they feel victorious when concluding the transaction and anxious to try them in the privacy of their settings, or surrounded by friends and family.

Sound can also become an important mood-setting factor; a loud, aggressive environment may deter purchasing, whereas a relaxing, melodic background tune may induce feelings of wellbeing, enhancing the willingness to buy.

Smells can be used to attract customers to acquire certain goods. Take, for instance, the characteristic McDonald's smell, surrounding their world-wide restaurants for a considerable distance; or even 5-star hotels, which have their lobbies, corridors and rooms lightly touched by a pleasurable, relaxing fragrance.

It is an interesting fact that structured polls, aiming at measuring the factors that determine the act of purchasing, often do not detect sensorial stimuli, simply because, consumers rarely remember them, upon providing their answers. In fact, for being emotional drivers, rather than logical ones, such stimuli are mainly processed at a subconscious level, and unconsciously associated with the purchase of a certain product; unless the poll is carefully designed to look for certain specific behaviours and actions, it may miss sensorial stimuli completely. To this date, several independent studies have confirmed that surroundings play an important part in the consumer's mind regarding the choice of store, point of sale, and of product.

Social Experiences outside home: The traditional marketplace has been a centre for social activities, where people gather to acquire goods and services, as well as to meet other people. All around the world, cities still hold 'market days' or specific 'fairs' and keep denominations such as 'market square' or 'marketplace' in their streets and alleys, in an effort to maintain alive a place for people to reunite and interact with one another. Even purely urban environments try to revive this tradition, holding street fairs, street events, shows and concerts, promoting themes, such as 'fashion weeks', 'arts and crafts exhibitions', auctions and so forth, to induce people to visit certain streets, stores or malls.

The most consumer-oriented stores, cluster of stores or malls have the responsibility of, apart from selling, carefully managing a busy events calendar, developing social, religious and recreational initiatives, some even with an educational or   professional approach, in an attempt to capture customers attention and willingness to visit -ultimately to make them purchase goods.

Going shopping (as an outside home exercise, not online shopping) is a social experience: to be able to provide an opportunity for engaging with other people, meeting friends and old acquaintances or to just observing passers-by.

Communicating with people with similar interests: Common interests constitute a privileged and most efficient manner of fostering communication between individuals and promoting social interaction. As such, many hobbies are centred on a specific product or service, such as sailing, collecting stamps, watching automobile events or home decorating. Stores offering products related to hobbies constitute attraction points for individuals with similar interests, wishing and willing to engage both the store clerks and other customers and share their points of view, experiences and doubts regarding their preferred activities.

Attraction by people with similar tastes: Being a customer of a certain store may serve the purpose of wanting to meet with people with similar tastes, or with a reference group one wished to belong. Record stores, for instance, are places where teenagers are usually found, whereas comic bookstores have a particular type of audience, where sci-fi fans can be met.

Establishments with specified target audiences take advantage of their customers to promote their business, often tapping into their preferences by holding specific promotions focussed on certain products or items, overall sales or simply by having the store clerks engaging customers in conversations aimed at determining the reasons behind the purchase of certain products. In addition, customers with certain preferences or members of certain groups with certain characteristics will be encouraged to visit the store, which in turn, will ensure that its colours, displays, sounds, smells, as well as products and services offerings are aligned with their customers' needs and expectations.

As illustrated by a variety of studies in this area, researchers concluded that the majority are less attracted to the store's surroundings - or even to its portfolio – than to the other individuals that can be found inside. These customers may even enter the store without any particular wish or desire to actually make a purchase, and many do not do so. Their desire to be associated with other customers, or the group they belong to or even with their preferences and likings, may constitute a powerful drive for disbursing money to acquiring products found inside.

Status and authority: Many shopping experiences provide an opportunity for gaining attention and respect from others. In fact, being a consumer – even if only a potential one - of products or services is an assurance of being 'served' by others, without having to pay – directly - for the service rendered. As such, it is possible to derive a sense of power and status in such a "master-servant"-type relationship, limited in scope, duration and confined to the store, which exists to "serve its target audience". To some, the joy triggered by feeling somehow superior may considerably delay – and sometimes even deter – the purchasing act, since once the item(s) have been paid for, the store clerk's attention will be channelled to a new potential customer.

Pleasure of bargaining: For a large number of consumers, bargaining is considered to be degrading. For others, however, it is a pleasurable and desired experience; these customers enjoy bargaining, believing that, engaging in a discussion over price with the salesperson may result in a much appreciated discount.

Apart from the competition between the buyer and the seller, bargaining elicits competition between buyers themselves, a battle of egos with the purpose of selecting the best shopper, capable of getting the best prices. In a transaction where prices are flexible, the act of bargaining will become a successful one whenever the buyer becomes convinced that others willing to acquire the same product will have to disburse a higher amount. In a fixed price transaction, the customer seeking to bargain will not become satisfied.

While the underlying motive to go shopping is tied to the need to purchase a product or acquire a service, the decision to go shopping will not be taken until the need for that product or service becomes important enough to justify the time, money and effort consumed in a trip to the store. Such a *planned purchase* will serve a double purpose: satisfying both the necessity fulfilled by the product or service as well the corresponding emotional and/or social need, as recognized by the consumer.

However, not all purchasing acts possess an underlying motivation. Such *unplanned*, or *impulse-driven*, purchases are not driven by any specific or previously identified needs, but rather by a series of random factors, from opportunity to convenience, from distance to the store to income availability, from the appeal of the store and surroundings, to its visual, sensorial and social attractiveness.

Accessibility, including transportation facilities are also important to entice consumers into visiting shopping establishments, thereby exposing them to endless shopping opportunities whilst on their way to work or to their social and/or leisurely activities.

Increased mobility emphasizes the existence of multiple alternatives to spend money, consequently improving the odds of performing an impulse-driven purchase.

CHAPTER 3

ADVERTISING CAMPAIGNS

In order to reveal their product and service offerings to the consumer, companies need to create and nurture an ongoing dialogue with their target. To do so, they rely on appropriate tools that enable them to adequately convey their brand, products and underlying concepts.

Promoting a product or a service starts with a conceptual and interpretative stage, which takes into account the product's features, benefits and positioning as well as the characteristics of the target or segment of the population to which it is primarily directed at.

In October 11th, 1996 the TV broadcast suddenly became glitched and soon interrupted. A problem with the network or with the power grid? No, just the new Renault Mégane Scénic campaign that took over all the TV channel advertising blocks! In an innovative and disruptive advertising campaign, Renault Portugal's advertising agency - Initiative Média - circumvented the usual channel surfing during commercial breaks and managed to capture the audience's attention with a TV spot that simulated a technical glitch, usually preceding an important newsflash. The news being, the launch of a new car model: the Mégane Scénic. The campaign was a success, driving sales of the model through the roof, with Renault Executives wanting to roll it out in other European countries.

This example illustrates how good advertising campaigns can be determinant in the success of sales; how a well planned, designed and implemented advertising campaign can be fundamental to capture audiences' attention and to communicate qualities and benefits associated with the purchasing of a product.

The advertising agency

Albeit numerous the reasons behind the choice of an advertising agency, its track record in terms of quality, efficiency and efficacy of previous campaigns is usually the decisive factor. Other criteria such as its human resources reputation, experience, skills and track record (with particular focus on the creative director and creative team), its annual revenues, its number and prestige of clients are considered to be not as relevant and issues like price bearing little importance.

Adirano Eliseu, a well-known Portuguese-Brazilian advertiser, stated in a recent interview that "it is a mistake for advertisers to believe that advertising agencies need to have an identity. An agency needs to create and strengthen an identity for the product it promotes; it is the product's necessity to possess and communicate its identity, not the agency's, if not for anything but for the simple reason that an agency, holding in its portfolio a wide variety of products, each with a specific identity, positioning and marketing strategy, must adapt itself to the demands and requirements of each product in its portfolio; must, at every time, and with every single product, become one with it, shifting demeanour, mindset, attitude, perspective to serve the product's best interests and become aligned with its values, motivations, objectives and goals, to better address the intended target segments and enhance market penetration and share whilst improving sales performance.

There are no *good* or *bad* agencies *per se*, as there are no *good* or *bad* clients on their own. Performance of the former is usually intimately related to that of the latter.

A good alignment between agency and client is paramount to the success of any campaign. Unfortunately, in some cases, parties find it hard to agree on issues, with agencies opting for producing extremely creative – and sometimes sterile – campaigns and clients demanding alterations – sometimes incongruent and completely orthogonal to the underlying positioning strategy. The result is a flawed communication message, with corresponding implications on sales and brand awareness.

Creativity without strategic support is gratuitous and random. Strategy without an underlying creative concept is barren. Clients – as well as final consumers - demand an advertising agency to provide a strategic response leveraged in market knowledge and to deliver a value proposition that uses a creative concept addressing the brand's needs and goals.

Fun, disruptive, innovative and inventive ideas are but a small element of the strategic process. They may lack relevance, applicability and, as such, have a negative impact on the promotional campaign. As an example, they may have a high impact in a very narrow timeframe and convey a *me-too image of the brand*, whereas its strategic goal aims at creating a highly differentiated positioning statement; they may use arguments directed at existing consumers, when it is the brand's desire to expand its market base and appeal to new and untapped segments.

As such, strategic - or marketing - objectives such as increasing sales, improving brand awareness or even capture new customers, need to be thoroughly translated into communication goals, in terms of both the message to convey as well as the audience to address, to lay solid and reliable guidelines and to follow an appropriate workframe during the creative stage. Strategic planning is a cold, clinical, analytical and a precise process. The more rigorous and encompassing it becomes the more support it will provide to downstream planning and development and the more successful the overall advertising campaign will, with greater probability, be.

Efficient and effective creativity must follow certain parameters or guidelines, among which, the following seven assume cardinal relevance:

Mastering knowledge of the product or service to be advertised;

Understanding the target segment(s), knowing its thoughts, recognizing its main processes guidelines, anticipating its reactions, being familiar with its interests and identifying its attitudes and perceptions towards the product or service to be advertised;

Being persuasive and convincing the customer of the urgency to acquire the product or service;

Allowing time for the customer to process the information;

Include technical information regarding the product or service features and characteristics, to flawlessly convey the message. As the famous pianist Paderewski used to say, 'art must always be preceded by technique".

Allowing for a learning process to take place both within the team responsible for creating the advertising campaign and inside the consumer's mind. According to Victor Ross, a known advertiser, "the a-ha!' moment usually comes from joining two apparently disconnected ideas";

Presenting the unexpected. Blurt Manning notes that an advertising campaign has high costs involved, and it can never be made successful when customers, bombarded with already expected and similar messages, tend to watch without really paying attention. The unexpected stimulates interest and curiosity, encouraging customers to remain attentive throughout the advertising piece and remembering it afterwards. The costs related to the usage of the "unexpected" are no greater than those pertaining to the expected and usual "themes" - expected concepts may even require higher repetition rates to sink in, and, therefore, higher running costs to attain the same goal.

One can ask the paradoxical question: does creativity really need to be effective and efficient? Is it not sufficient to design extraordinarily creative advertising pieces for the campaign to become a success, translated into higher sales? An agency that only delivers extremely creative pieces may be doing a disservice to its clients, as many other less original solutions, sometimes much more adequate to the product/service and/or target segment in question, yield better overall results in a way where they are also better serving the client's needs and aspirations. If this is so, why are less original solutions not used that often? Agencies delivering advertising pieces with little or no supporting creative innovation are often shunned by fellow professionals, sometimes demeaned and even hated to a point of becoming banned from competitions. But the fact remains that such campaigns can – and have - become a large success with customers, which feel driven and motivated by the advertising piece, considering it to be a determining factor behind the purchase decision.

Advertising should not be conceived by a small elite of pseudo-intellectual advertisers, but to take into account that the ultimate judge of an advertising campaign is the target customer and its final verdict, together with the product or service annual sales report.

Creativity followed by a profound knowledge of the market, of the client, of the product/service and of the cost/deliverables are the four main factors considered to be determinant to the choice of an advertising agency – this was the conclusion of a study conducted by Secches, targeting Portuguese companies resorting to advertising agencies to promote their products or services. However, and despite the broad range of services offered by advertising agencies creativity still continues to be the primordial driver for choosing an agency, according to 62% of respondents.

The advertising campaign

Upon designing an advertising campaign, agencies usually denote great care when choosing the elements or key ingredients that will be part of the communication piece:

Language: Language is a symbolic set used for communication, for translating emotions, feelings and ideas into rational and logically organized statements. Each word is represented by a symbol and text blocks confer meaning to the words. The symbol is a natural expression of the myth, of both the sacred and the social, of the economic and of all human activity – it is not universally objective.

In a society where every object, being, action and aspiration has a symbolic counterpart, any successful advertising piece must seek to be colonized with the appropriate symbols, those that will effectively address the specific and intended target segments.

Music: The need to overcome barriers - cultural, religious, idiomatic or even functional - call for the use of music as an aggregating unifying element. To Aslam Shems, from India-based advertising agency Shems Combit, "music is a bridge connecting cultures separated by rivers of differences".

Sound: Audio is the last element to be inserted in the advertising piece. The decision of developing an original soundtrack over choosing a catalogue piece is a very wise course of action. Catalogue pieces are widely used in a variety of situations, deterring audiences from forming indelible and lasting associations with the product or service being promoted by the advertising spot using database tracks as audio support.

Original soundtracks, being unique and purposely developed with the product or service in mind, can easily be remembered by consumers and permanently associated with the product, and immediately, involuntarily and unconsciously be recalled whenever the tune is heard or remembered.

Choosing a voice that will feature in an advertising piece is also an important decision to be made. Attributes such as vocal register, pitch, tone, modulation, volume, timbre and vibration must be carefully considered and matched to, or aligned with, the product's or service's positioning and respective target segments. Often, and because of the high demand from producers, creative Directors and also from the clients themselves, the most sought after voices may appear in two consecutive – and unrelated – advertising spots, which is highly undesirable, since it may create random associations between products or services.

In order to circumvent the tendency to cast the usual actors, producers are known to take risks and hire unknown professionals to play the part. Taking into account the tight deadlines, the multiplicity of teams, people and partners involved as well as the high costs associated with the making of an advertising campaign, producers will most often prefer an experienced and reliable actor to voice the ad instead of a first-timer, a newcomer in need of coaching and time to get things done the right way – a luxury that, in advertising, may cost a significant sum of money.

In Portugal, voice casting is performed primarily by radio and theatre professionals; a new tendency is emerging, whereby producers are choosing to bring on board what Manuel Faria labelled as 'voice models' or 'voice extras', in an analogy to what is usually made in the film industry, where untrained people have walk-in parts side-by-side with the seasoned movie stars, to add diversity and colour to the piece. In this manner, Portuguese ads are combining seasoned, perfectly pitched and articulated voices with young, insecure, harsh, funny, gentile, hip, nasal ones, resulting in a most efficient mixture of styles and genres, appealing to both clients and customers.

Silence: Mental and Physical health requires silence, which is used as a tool to convey and enhance certain aspects of the advertising message, or characteristics of the product or service being promoted. The absence of sound, for prolonged periods of time may become aggressive and promote stressful situations - Why is there no sound? Why can't I hear anything? Is there something wrong with my radio or TV? These are questions listeners and viewers may pose if a certain advertising spot exceeds its 'quiet time' by a second or two. In some cases, silence can become more harmful than noise, sometimes it may even be made oppressive, especially in situations commonly identified and associated with specific sounds. Imagine a bar, filled with people during Happy Hour, around 6 p.m. Now, imagine, the minute you walk in the door, that not a single sound is heard: no talking or laughing; no tinkling of glasses; no football playing in the dimly lit TV; no shuffling of stools...

Image: Images express emotions, define ideas, symbolize an abstract concept, tell a story or depict a preference. From the moment a creative director decides which image to use, it must be obtained without further delays, as it will serve as a guideline, a backbone around which the advertising piece will be developed.
The advertising spot cannot by itself promote a product. It needs to be supported by an image, intimately

associated to the brand or the product; it creates a strong impression and a lasting memory.

Image storing is an activity that goes back to the American Civil War, where, for the first time, a photographer recording images on the battlefield decided to sell them to a local newspaper, for information purposes. However, it wasn't until 1900, that the use of stocked images started to bloom in Europe. In 1940, the USA acknoledge the use of stock images as a valuable tool for the press industry. Magazines such as *Life* and *Look* and newspapers such as *The Saturday Evening Post* also realized that images could be resold to unspecified users, working in other industries and began taking action in promoting and developing the image stock business.

In 1974, *Image Bank* entered the market to become what today is (probably) the largest image stockpiler in the world. Serving a variety of customers, public, corporate and private players within commercially-oriented areas and with special focus on the advertising industry - this company embarked in a successful image stock management business, which has become a reference worldwide, providing access, in exchange for a small fee, to the rights of use of images, and lately, to video compositions.

Shocking content: A man is sitting quietly on a park bench. Suddenly he starts hearing protests, which become louder more intense, and rapidly turn into screams of rage, of helplessness, of despair. A young girl is being raped in the vicinity, while shouting for help, in an attempt to free herself from her abuser. Terrified with the idea of becoming involved, the man gets up and rapidly heads home, running fast, without looking back. As soon as he crosses the threshold of his apartment, he feels his palms are wet, maybe sweaty. He looks down and finds his hands are dripping blood! *"Doing Nothing is Taking Part"* is the shocking message of this advertising spot, entitled "Bloody Palms" from Spring & Jakoby/Hamburg, for the 1998 *Public Services* category. The client was the Police Department, the aim, to encourage a less passive attitude towards crime.

Erotic and Sensual contents: It is a delicate issue to choose an erotic approach when promoting a product. However, if performed with intelligence and tastefulness, it may become a widely accepted success.
The genesis of sexual desire was firstly understood by a team of French researchers and published in the *Archives of Sexual Behaviour*, identifying five regions in the brain, which register enhanced activity whenever sexual arousal takes place. The team used positron emission tomography imaging, or PET scans, to search for differences in brain activity before, during and after sexual arousal of subjects, male and female, and concluded that the brain's activation is performed in

five different regions, prior to any action taking place: the first region lights up when the brain decodes the images the subject is viewing (the volunteers were shown movies), the second, as the brain assesses the pleasure in the viewing, the third, as it triggers physical responses in other parts of the body, such as an accelerated heart frequency and an erection, the fourth when the subject becomes conscientious of the situation, and the fifth, when the subject decides to take action.

Today's world is extremely sexualized. The use of sexual/erotic-content advertising may be an issue in many parts of the world, due to social, moral or even religious restrictions. Such is the case of Muslim countries, whereby women are not allowed to feature in advertising pieces, except in well-defined socially and religiously approved contexts. In Saudi Arabia, for instance, restrictions to advertising – as expressed in the Censorship Code - force agencies to abide by Muslim values and create pieces that are fundamentally different from those exhibited in the west. In fact, according to TV advertising guidelines, during the 90's, women in Saudi Arabia could only feature in TV spots if depicted in situations concerning household duties, such as dusting, cleaning, ironing, cooking and taking care of children, and, at all times, they needed to exhibit modesty in words, tone of voice, appearance, movement and overall demeanour. For advertising agencies with clients in Saudi Arabia, devising or merely adapting a piece to suit Islamic sensibilities can be a challenge. Amongst the various cares to be taken into account, it is necessary that shoulders, arms and legs be covered or that female faces be kept outside the frame. During Ramadan, restrictions are made even more severe, with women being unable to star in advertisements of any kind.

Investment in local televisions has been loosing ground for satellite-broadcast channels, which allow for better and wider network coverage. In local stations, shows and advertising are highly controlled by the government, to ensure abidance to Muslim values. Despite such difficulties, in 1995, numbers indicated that the Saudi advertising business yielded over 270 Million dollars in revenues, the highest value in the Middle East, according to the Pan Arab Research Centre, with forecasts predicting growth for the next few years.

Homosexuality and bisexuality: During advertising festivals, there is always something new, unexpected and different. There are movements, allegiances and, most importantly, ideas that work and are capable to strengthen or even change attitudes towards products. Whenever ideas are echoed in the minds of consumers, they drive trends and actions. This is clearly the case of homosexuality and bisexuality.

For a long time regarded as taboo, especially in advertising pieces wishing to be forward but without imposing on audience's sensitivities, homosexuality, and bisexuality, is definitively a reality nowadays. George Michael, in his 1987 "*I want your Sex*" video clip, ridiculed those who still had negative thoughts regarding *gay power*. Since then, advertisers grabbed on to the chance of enlargement the breadth and depth of their pieces by exploring such themes in fun, expressive and influential manners. An example is London Ogilvy & Mather's Justin Hooper and Christian Cotterill pieces "Orgia", for Fusion, illustrating, in a soft, smooth manner, several types of sexual preferences, or "Encounter", for Elida Fabergé, denoting a sound example of *gay culture*, depicting tolerance in an evermore understanding and inclusive society.

Dark Humour: This kind of humour still echoes strongly in many European countries, especially in France and in the UK. In a British ad, an extremely successful man is shown. Although hated by all, his life is a perfect one, filled with all a man could ask for – and more. One day, as he is walking by, a piano comes out of nowhere and falls on top of him. A voice is heard "*sorry!*" said by someone standing at the ledge of a window, several storeys high, evidently the one responsible for dropping the piano on the successful entrepreneur…and he is drinking a Royco-Cup-A-Soup, with a warm smile on his face. In another ad, some sort of circus/carnival fair has come to town. A Jamaican man throws a heavy iron ball into the air and it falls down on an irritating little poodle, owned by an equally irritating and uptight lady, who starts screaming her lungs out. Back to the Jamaican, who says, "Don't worry", while taking a relaxed bite off his Mars bar.

Simple Ideas: According to Geoff Thomson, award winning humour is universal humour. Looking at Cannes advertising festival where the most representative pieces worldwide are paraded, it is generally the simple ideas that reap the most coveted awards and yield the most wanted results.

Perfection of nature: Contrasting with simple arguments, some advertising pieces can be made extremely complex, but still become very successful, as, towards the end, all apparently disconnected elements start falling into their rightful places. Quietly. Perfectly. Harmoniously. Imparting a sense of completeness to the advertisement. An example is Z. Publicidade's A-Class Mercedes Benz *'Crash Test'* film, for Mercedes-Benz Portugal, where collisions between cars and people – men, women, children and even a baby stroller were exhibited in black-and-white and in slow motion to the sound of a child-sang nursery rhyme. Another example is Reebok's ad, where sepia-coloured images depicted real-life situations, such as that of a basketball player shooting hoops in a desert where it suddenly starts to rain, to the sound of a classical track. Another example is TBWA/London's *"it just grows on you"* for PlayStation, imagining a human being with amplified sensorial abilities, short listed for "Épica" awards in 1998.

Laughter: Laughter is a unique privilege of the human race; according to Harvard University psychology professor William McDougall, "… laughter has the added proven benefit of preserving both physical and mental well-being". This is not, of course, a new idea. Back in the 17th century, British physicist Thomas Sydenhman stated, "a clown coming to this town would do more good to its inhabitants than twenty donkeys with saddlebags filled with medicine". Years later, Sigmund Freud bestowed on laughter the power to free one's organism of negative energy, which later was confirmed by scientific research studies which prove how the brain cortex – the area covering both brain hemispheres – releases electrical pulses shortly after the onset of laughter, stimulating pleasurable responses.

Stanford's University William Fry concluded, after extensive research, that creativity is related to good humour. This specialist has proven that children laugh, in average, around 300 times a day, until the age of six, a time when education and social pressures restrain their will to laugh and refrain their willingness to express joy. According to the *Associação Internacional para a Renovação do Riso* (International Association for the Renewal of Laughter), whilst in 1930 an adult would laugh, in average, for a total period of about nineteen minutes every day, in 1980 he/she would laugh for only six minutes, and in 1990 for a mere three minute interval.

Studies have shown that, the more advanced a culture is, the less time it spends on laughter. A challenge to authority and to the established social order, laughter has become almost banned from acceptable social behaviours in certain contexts and situations. In Oscar Wilde's words, "the world has always laughed at its own tragedies, that being the only way in which it has been able to bear them".

Superstition: Black cats terrified Napoleon Bonaparte; Socrates was obsessed by the evil eye; Julius Caesar feared dreams and Henry VIII claimed Anne Boleyn had cast a spell to force their marriage...and even to this date the creation of the world still bears elements of magic and superstition to societies, even the most evolved ones. In the US, some states still swear beside creationism, while in Italy, coins are thrown inside fountains, for luck.

Psychologists claim that people believe in superstitions because, when facing the unknown, they feel safer and more protected than they would otherwise, and therefore, increase their chances of a favourable outcome. "Since certain things cannot be rationally / logically explained, or controlled in a deterministic fashion, they automatically elapse in a kind of dimensional gap, or reality breach, filled with magic and beliefs that grant protection to those who follow simple guidelines", explains Victor Cotovio, psychiatrist at Casa de Saúde do Telhal, a clinical facility specializing in mental illnesses.

Specialists define superstitions as the need for a belief in something that brings meaning to things the human being cannot fully understand. Whenever a rational and logical explanation cannot be found, myth and superstition provide an answer.

According to writer Charles Panati, M.D., the first superstition was recorded around 50 000 BC by the early Neanderthals, in west Asia, who believed in the existence of something beyond their daily existence; while the Homo Sapiens abandoned their dead, the Neanderthal would carefully bury the departed with clothing, weapons, food, coal and ornaments, to be used in an afterlife.

Historians believe that primitive men surrounded by numerous perils and facing severe hardships have developed a system of beliefs and rites, to which superior powers were attributed, destined to protect their lives and their meagre possessions. With time, these beliefs and rites have been adapted by civilizations and included in their social and religious behaviours. For example, during the Middle Ages, the number of existing beliefs and superstitions was extremely high due to the survival of pagan customs and rites, not fully and successfully extinguished by the ruling Catholic Church. Historian Jean Claude Smitt maintains the theory that it was the obsession some clergymen had with such presumable supernatural powers that led to the dissemination of the belief in witches and witchcraft, and to the aggressive actions and relentless persecution performed by the Church – or in its name - against innocent men and women.

For centuries, life continued to be hard, especially for country people, more exposed to and more dependants on weather conditions and other seemingly unexplainable natural occurring phenomena or unforeseen events. The birth of new cities and the development of cultural and social exchanges between different people with different origins and backgrounds allowed for the exchange of information and for an overall improvement in education; superstition could no longer remain as strong, since it was possible to find reasonable and perfectly sound explanations to what was previously attributed to external magical entities. The rationalism brought forth by the "Century of Lights" was the *coup de grace* for superstitions, transformed into mere banalities, curious facts and pleasant stories to be told to children.

Whilst the majority of western civilizations have abandoned most superstitions – or swept some of its beliefs under the cloak of religion – other cultures have strived to keep them alive as an integral part of their roots and traditions. Such is the case of countries like Japan, or China - highly superstitious - and also of Germany, or certain regions of Brazil, or Greece, India, or even France or Portugal, where superstitious customs can still be observed.

Bad fortune

Most remaining superstitions can provide explanations to justify the occasional unfortunate turn of events.

Sweeping the feet of a single woman or a widow: Indicates they would nor get married or remarried, respectively. This superstition takes its origins from the fact that witches, bearers of misfortune, would have broomsticks as their elected means of transportation.

Opening an umbrella indoors: This belief goes back to 18th century Britain, whereupon it was a general belief that such an action would bring great misfortune, since negative energies would be able to flow inside the house through the opened umbrella, given that the household spirits would be extremely crossed in having an alien object – the umbrella – protecting its inhabitants, a task only "the house" should perform. The superstition was taken even further, by claiming that, if a person were to open an umbrella indoors, over his or her head, then he or she would be dead within the year.

Spilling salt: Dating back from 3 500 BC, when salt was believed to be incorruptible, as it was commonly used as a preserver, and considered to be a symbol of friendship, it should not be wasted – or spilled, lest the friendship end. Upon inadvertently spilling salt, one should try and nullify the mishap, by throwing another pinch of the substance over one's left shoulder.

Black Cat: In ancient Egypt, the cat was considered to be an incarnation of the goddess Bastet, but centuries later, the Catholic Church considered the animal to be the reincarnation of the devil himself, for being the colour of the night, having had many of these creatures burned at the stake. In northern America and throughout Europe it is believed that a black cat will bring good fortune to a person if it walks towards that person, and bad fortune if otherwise.

Starting off with the left foot: Petronius, in his

masterpiece *Satyricon*, made reference to the bad fortune bestowed upon those who would enter a place with their left foot. In Portugal, reminiscent of Celtic tradition attributes this superstition to the solar movement, performed towards the right, a direction symbolizing righteousness, natural harmony and alignment with the universe. Entering a place with the left foot somehow breaks with the established natural order and brings bad fortune. By blessing oneself three consecutive times, the negative effect can be reverted.

Friday, the 13th: To the Christian world, the curse brought forth by the number thirteen derives from Christ's last supper, where he broke bread with twelve of his apostles before being betrayed, which led to his cruel death on the cross. It is believed that if thirteen people sit at a table to eat, one of them will die within a year. The 'unlucky' day of the week, associated to the thirteenth day as a major bearer of misfortune varies from country to country. In Portugal, as well as in Anglo-Saxon territories Friday is the most feared day of the week, for being that when Jesus was crucified, while in Spain and Mexico, Tuesday the Thirteenth is the day to avoid.

Breaking a mirror: Popular wisdom states this action will bring seven years of bad luck. The mirror was considered to be a magical divination object. It broke whenever it attempted to show an image of the future, one so terrifying and filled with such unimaginable horrors that made it impossible for the glass to hold itself together. Seven years is also the time taken for a body to supposedly renew itself.

Walking under a ladder: The ladder forms a triangle with the floor and with the wall it stands against. It was believed that triangles were sacred symbols, a conviction manifested in architecture – such as is the case of the Egyptian pyramids – in secret societies – such as the masonry – in religion – as with the Holy Trinity and even in primitive cultures, where the triangle represented the female womb, and with it femininity, fertility and prosperity. As such, it was considered sacrilegious to cross triangles or triangle-shaped obstacles. To undo the possible effects of such wrongdoing, it is necessary to cross one's fingers and spit under the ladder, or, in alternative, to spit three times under the ladder.

The evil eye: It was widely believed that, by starring into the pupil of someone's eye, one could become forever ensorcelled under that someone's spell. Since ancient Rome and throughout the middle ages, people suffering from cataracts or other visual impairments were usually burnt at the stake.

Sleeping in a bed with one's feet facing the door: As

the saying goes, "the dead always leave a room feet first".

Good fortune

Most beliefs pertaining to good fortune have their genesis in the human need to control unforeseen and unpredictable future events:

Chicken bones: 2 400 years ago, it was believed that roosters – chanting to the rising of a new dawn - and hens – crying when laying eggs - both possessed some sort of divine power over mere mortals, and that their bones had the magical ability of granting wishes.

Crossing fingers: Before Christian ages, people used to cross their index fingers forming a cross, to express a wish. One finger would represent the wish and the other would support the former, so that the wish is granted. The cross, in pre-Christian times, was seen as a symbol of perfection and the point where the segments united, an abode for good spirits. Nowadays, the cross has been replaced by a simple crossing of fingers.

Saying 'Bless you' or 'Gesundheit' whenever someone sneezes: Despite involuntary, sneezing was – and is - an action that favoured the spreading of diseases; as such, whenever someone sneezes, it is usual to ask God to protect those who are healthy from contracting the disease. It is also said that it prevented the devil from entering the diseased person's body through the mouth.

Hanging a horseshoe behind the door: According to the Greek, a half-moon-shaped piece of iron would serve as a protection against spells. Hanging a horseshoe on the door would protect the home against witches and evil. The luckiest horseshoes were those of small donkeys, because they had seven holes, with seven being considered the most magical of all numbers.

Four-leaved clove: A sacred symbol for Britannia-dwelling druids, who used four-leaved cloves to see demons. Also, when cast from Paradise, Eve left with a four-leaved clove in her hand, and, since then, the plant is believed to be a bearer of good fortune.

Throwing coins inside a well or in a fountain: Goes back to the ancient rite of throwing pins or pebbles inside a well, as a means of guessing whether a certain event would come to pass. If, upon falling, the object would draw air bubbles at the surface of the water, then the outcome would be favourable.

Touching wood: A possible origin for this superstition may come from Christian tradition, whereby touching the wood from the Holy Cross would bring good fortune. Another possible explanation comes from the US, where native American Indians worshipped the oak tree as a place inhabited by the gods, 4 000 years ago.

Rabbit's foot: Every culture possesses an animal with divine characteristics, which could not be hunted down and killed by men, for food. In India, it's the cow. To most western civilizations, the rabbit assumes that role. A rabbit's foot also served as a phallic symbol, capable of making women become fertile.

Superstitions possess a great cultural and social impact, varying from latitude to longitude and depending on the economical and educational characteristics of populations, as well as their lifestyles and system of beliefs. Nowadays, the most superstitious populations are found in China, in central Europe and among Mediterranean regions, partly due to the survival, to these days, of ancient traditions. Northern Europeans are considered to be less gullible, considering the rationality their culture usually exhibits.

The nature of superstitious beliefs also depends on geography. In North America, the evil eye is regarded with extreme fear, as so is every Friday, the 13th. Touching wood is a common procedure and the oak tree is usually treated with respect.

In Europe, superstitions are common throughout the majority of countries, with exception of the UK and Ireland, where beliefs are much more intense. It was in the UK where the search for four-leaved cloves started, where the fear of fowl emerged, where opening umbrellas inside buildings became shunned.

In the East, the fearing the evil eye is common. In eastern Russia, horseshoes are bearers of an exaggerated magical power, such that the blacksmith was once considered a wizard of white magic and judgements and weddings were performed over a blacksmith's anvil.

CHAPTER 4

THE ELDERLY SEGMENT

To Peter Drucker, it is an absurd to say that the world's population will double soon. In fact, the world's population has already reached a point where it has attained a maximum in numbers, soon to be decreasing. The main reason that will explain the decrease in population is the enormous workload imposed on the younger active generations, in order to support the older, retired ones, still exhibiting a perfect bill of health. Europeans are trying to cut on expenses as much as possible, in seemingly Darwinian survival tactics.

According to the author, retirement age will tend to evolve towards 75 years of age, in most developed countries, since people, at this age, should still have the abilities and health to perform accurately and efficiently. "If retirement age would be pushed up to 75 years, golf courts and the most well-known resorts would become empty", states the author.

Europeans are getting old. There are less and less children and more single people, either young bachelors and bachelorettes deciding to postpone marriage in favour of a better and more successful career or widowers deciding to live alone. The population has become more urban and available time has become evermore important due to its scarcity.

The segment composed by mature people – with ages above 65 – is vast and extremely interesting, thus becoming an appealing and attractive target for both companies and advertisers.

The end of the 20th century brings a change in paradigm: instead of focussing exclusively on young, active people, more sensitive to fast food, sodas and jeans-peddling, we see advertising shifting towards silver surfers, bringing forth advertising pieces promoting senior residences, continuous learning products and other goods targeting a more educated, richer, healthier and older segment. Engaging the elderly segment must be performed taking into account its specific and unique characteristics, which determine contents, imagery, language and music, without which the communication may not attain its communication objectives.

Although it may be an overstatement to say that all members of a certain age group go through the exact same changes, in body and in mind, it is nevertheless a fact that such changes remain relatively similar within certain parameters. One day, we too will get old and that is an uncontroverted truth. As such, it is important to understand which factors are determinant for – or may affect – elderly people to grasp the full meaning of the advertising messages conveyed to them.

Nervous stimuli received by any part of the body is immediately processed by the brain and translated into meaningful information; this, in turn, is rapidly apprehended and stored. This perception-learning process is subject to a series of parameters and bodily functions, which naturally decay with age. As the body gets older, the acquisition of information will suffer changes, which need to be carefully taken into account upon designing effective promotional campaigns aiming at this mature segment.

To begin with, advertising messages must be kept simple otherwise they may not be fully retained. Also, they must not be overloaded with information as its apprehension may constitute a tiresome and an inglorious challenge. Furthermore, it is fundamental that the advertising message is supported by a series of familiar concepts, with a strong rational and logical background, minimizing abstrac and elaborated trains of thought when possible.

The use of explicit language is paramount, especially when conveying the main purpose or idea of the piece;

it should always be chosen over implicit concepts or hidden meanings.

The initial stimulus should be made as strong as possible and preferentially include the most important information to be delivered, since it is this initial nudge that will cause the lasting impression on the subject. Lastly, written supports, or supports that include printed messages should be considered since this is prone to impart a more profound impression on the audience, one less likely to become easily forgettable.

The body's memory system handles recognition and recall of events, situations, people, objects, messages and so forth, by linking them to daily tasks and familiar things. In order to effectively communicate with elderly people, any form of dialogue must be correctly and carefully framed, either by using specific leads or triggers, or by choosing adequate contextualization of concepts and ideas, so that the message can be fully apprehended and later recalled. For instance, visual leads are more successfully remembered than audio leads or isolated syllables and should be used as memory tools - aiding verbal expressions like "it's just as" (queuing visual imaging) or "it's simply like" to convey and anchor the underlying concept. Also, whenever an advertising message makes use of the subject's memories or remembrances, appropriate images must be chosen, accompanied by words pointing to the subject's own lifelong references, such as "do you remember your…" or "imagine your…", which constitute effective support mechanisms of recollection.

The elderly segment possesses unique needs and demands, which can be fully explored by advertisers when defining a promotional campaign, such as:

Comfort: The necessity for comfort is a priority among older people;

Safety: The implicit need for safety is known to increase with age;

Convenience: Making life easy - older people attribute more value to products or services which make their daily routines simpler and less troublesome;

Sense of duty and of purpose: Older people possess an enormous need to live up to what is expected of them - regardless of these expectations being externally or internally driven, as well as to feel useful to others;

Social Networking: A reliable group of friends sharing similar interests or preferences is of the utmost importance to this segment, favouring situations that can provide opportunities of social interaction;

Independence: Elderly people dislike having to impose on others, and value situations and activities which they can perform on their own;

Sensuality and romance: There are several marketing opportunities aiming at the satisfaction of this need. Sex, romance and desire are as legitimate – and as important - wants for the elder as are other needs, such as eating, walking and sleeping.

The "Last Voyage": With age, people tend to place more importance on spiritual issues, and the concept of a "hereafter" or of a "final destination" assumes a relevant dimension;

Heroes/Inspirational models: Successful elders are role models to others in similar situations. Ageing gracefully while maintaining an active and dynamic lifestyle can be used to distil positive and inspirational values that may inspire others to follow;

Experience: To induce feelings related to the experience of being;

Nostalgia: Nostalgic themes constitute an extremely effective positioning approach as they associate the concept of familiarity with products and services.

Apart from the points above, which find greater echo with the elderly segment, it is also important, when conceiving an advertising piece aimed at silver surfers, to carefully considerate other aspects of the marketing mix, to better promote communication and foster consumption, such as:

Product: Elders require specific products/services tailored to the needs of the age group they belong by taking into account the biological changes to their body and mind, as well as their available free time, income and respective interests;

Price: Elders usually possess a high sensitivity towards price, often comparing prices of similar products or of products in similar categories. As such, this segment is an ideal target for price or price-penetration strategies, or even for generic brand portfolio launches.

Distribution: Great concerns should be placed upon accessibility, comfort, safety and convenience. Access routes must be clearly shown and product displays easily found. Also, parking spots for elderly people must be made available at short distances from the entrances to the stores or shopping malls. As should transportation to and from stores, to drive older people to shopping facilities. Access barriers and obstacles, stairs, steps as well as heavy doors should be avoided.

CHAPTER 5

PLANNING AN ADVERTISING CAMPAIGN

When planning an advertising campaign, following the initial briefing conveyed by the client, agencies usually hold brainstorming sessions, bringing together the team members that will be involved in the promotion of the product or service. Creatives, marketing strategists, media planners and account managers will sit together and start the creative thought process from which the advertising piece will emerge.

Brainstorming is a group meeting technique intended to aid participants in overcoming self imposed barriers promoting unconventional, out-of-the-box, innovative thinking without restrictions or constraints. Created by Osborn in 1963, a brainstorming session may last from a few minutes to several hours, according to the participants and the subject matter to discuss. When brainstorming, it is essential to keep in mind four golden rules: never to criticize a suggestion, as awkward or silly as it may be, always to encourage bizarre and wild ideas, to prefer quantity to quality and finally never to respect intellectual property.

It is a curious fact that children can constitute excellent consultants in creativity. Companies like Microsoft, Levi's Strauss and MTV have been using 'young' advisors for designing and launching campaigns and promotional spots, using children's creativity to promote associations between words, objects, situations and feelings in a brainstorming-type interactions and interviews.

Upon creating a campaign it is necessary to take into account several factors that can determine its success – or demise – bearing a significant impact on the campaign's awareness, spontaneous or assisted, as well as on the mental positioning of the product, with respect to the consumers hierarchy of preferences.

Some experts consider a high level of awareness of an advertising piece to be a synonym of efficacy; in other words, if an advertisement is noticed and remembered by consumers, then sales of the respective product should rise. In reality, this statement is not entirely truthful, since there are examples of advertising spots that had a large impact on audiences, some even still remembered by a majority of people, but which did not result in a desired increase in sales of the product. In such cases, the advertising piece has not been able to influence consumers into actually making a purchase; in other words, it has not been able to influence the expected consumer behaviour.

How many times have we been outdoors, away from out TV set and heard the jingle of a familiar commercial....and although we know we have heard it over and over again, we still cannot bring to mind the products it is promoting, or the name of the brand being advertised? Along with the jingle, images start flashing in front of our eyes, bringing forth feelings of warmth, cold, joy, happiness, disdain, and disgust... Suddenly we remember the entire advertisement, from beginning to end. The people acting in it, their clothes, the dog, the car, the sky, the hot coffee pot, the melting butter on the toast, the rapture of the perfume the pretty girl is wearing...What was the name of the product again? Many times, wee cannot remember. For one reason or another, the film was impressed in our memory, but an indelible association to the product was not made.

In December 1999, one Portuguese TV channel showed a film in which a couple was wreaking havoc in their home; a game of seduction, desire, romance and passion leading to destruction and total annihilation, with a powerful pounding soundtrack for background: a perfect connection between image and sound. But Bruit, the customer, still did not sell its perfume. A later poll suggested that audiences recognized the images and linked them to the music, but not to the product or the brand.

Another example is the advertising spot created for branded deodorant AXE, wherein a man, a flute player, after succeeding in driving each and every single mouse from town and being denied payment for his services, decided to spray his deodorant over the city, having its inhabitants fall into a passionate trance. Albeit its visual and audio impact, this spot did not perform well for the product. People remembered the man, the flute, the mice and the music, but had no clue as to which product was being advertised.

Campaigns must therefore be carefully thought of and planned, in order to efficiently promote both the brand and the product, whilst increasing their awareness among audiences and promoting consumption; the worse output is when the campaign output becomes a simple promotional vehicle for the piece itself, or the agency that executed the advertisement. Besides wasting precious resources, bringing forth inefficient campaigns may ultimately result in the client dismissing the advertising agency, as per what has happed with Subaru.

Before the consecutive disappointing results in sales,

Subaru decided to shift advertising agencies, having chosen Wieden & Kennedy, a reputed, new-age risk-taking agency from Oregon handling the Nike account.

The resulting clash between two utterly distinct organizational cultures and positionings eventually proved to be fatal for both partners. While Subaru's objectives were focused on recovering market share, Wieden & Kennedy was interested in creating intelligent; out-of-the-box adverts. During this engagement period, and until parties ended their relationship not agreeing on strategies nor on actions, Subaru kept accumulating losses.

Agency-client Relationship management

There is no mathematical equation that can determine the relationship between the quality of a certain advertisement and the sales increase corresponding to the product it promotes. What several studies have ascertained though, is that advertisement is a driver for sales. As such, there is room for tension between client and agency, the former believing the campaign produced will yield the expected results and the latter wanting prove that it will happen so.

The advent of technology-powered interactive campaigns has managed to provide data that allows correlations to be made between advertisement and sales. Note that even with the most up-to-date tequiques, there is always a margin for error, which must be taken into account when planning a campaign.

It is fundamental for both the agency and the client to understand the specific target audience, its preferences and characteristics in order to define an advertising concept that is not only adequate to the consumer but also consistent with brand guidelines.

CHAPTER 6

INTERNATIONAL ALIGNMENT VS. LOCAL STRATEGY

Some years ago, the buzz word was globalization and shared strategies. For reasons tied to cost effectiveness and global planning, some products possessed a similar – if not equal – positioning, promotional strategy and price levels in a variety of countries.

According to Rosabeth Moss Kanter, information technologies, or IT, brought forth a truly global village, a concept rapidly adopted by managers as a synonym for the worldwide integration of all activities developed by an organization, where resources, processes and budgets are defined globally and then passed down to local structures.

Theodore Levitt was the first guru to shed some light upon the global homogeneity of customer preferences. In a 1960 Harvard Business Review piece, the author introduced the concept of *Marketing*

Myopia, in which it is the industry itself, and not the goods or services it manufactures or distributes, the main driver for customer satisfaction, and that all products can be sold at a global scale, under the umbrella of a global brand, due to the progressive homogeneity in terms of customer preferences and purchasing habits.

The onset of the European Common Market introduced normative requirements, in which standards were set for almost each and every category of products and services available. This, in turn, fuelled the importance of international alignments; since goods and services were required to present uniform overall characteristics regardless of where they were produced, manufactured, distributed and sold, as well as similar price levels, it followed that promotion and communication strategies should be maintained equal. According to João Belo, in a world made increasingly smaller and without room for so-called traditional lifestyles, isolated from the frantic information society in which we live in, it seems inevitable that advertising is, evermore, a transcultural activity.

There are many examples of successful international alignment strategies, carefully planned and cautiously implemented that became exciting case studies taught at business schools all around the world. Such is the case for Sanex, the shower gel developed by Spanish Cruz-Verde Legraín, local subsidiary of the multinational Sara Lee Corporation. Following a successful launch in Spain during the mid-nineties, the product revolutionized the *Household & Body Care* category, fuelling the competitive dynamics of the market which saw a dramatic increase in sales sustained for several years. Expansion to other European territories seemed an appropriate business decision and it was decided that the same advertising campaign would be rolled out, using the same positioning and promotional message: "Dermoprotection at an affordable price available at a nearby supermarket".

UK's refusal in launching the product with the international alignment adopted by other countries, opting instead for a local strategy, considered to be more in tune with British preferences and lifestyle, was a proved flop, forcing the withdrawal of the product from the market; the shower gel, re-named 'Santé' in UK territories simply would not sell.

The subsequent re-launch of the product, following the 'Sanex concept' and initial communication strategy was to become a success.

Other brands, such as tobacco companies Philip Morris, Camel or Winston, as well as multinational corporations like Nestlé or General Motors also rely on a single promotional strategy deployed worldwide or directed at a specific continent, usually working with a single advertising agency, which centralizes the planning and execution of the promotional campaign, handing it down to local subsidiaries for small adaptations, like language-specific audio or visual contents.

It should, however, be noted that, in some cases, a global strategy may not be a wise choice. More often than not, it is necessary to perform small changes and alterations to the planned advertisements in order to match local preferences. In some situations, it may even be necessary to completely reformulate the entire promotional campaign to achieve the desired goals in terms of awareness, market share and, last but not least, sales. In fact, taking into account that no two identical markets exist, it can be argued that shopping habits and consumer behaviour are as unique as fingerprints and, as such, there are specific products and services that require a careful geographic segmentation in order to meet both the client's as well as the market's expectations.

Take for instance the case of India, with an enormous diversity of provinces, languages – around sixteen - religious confessions and so forth. No wonder that foreign advertising agencies, when operating in the country, often resort to local teams, immersed in the local habits, versatile in the local mannerisms and knowledgeable of the local cultural heritage and traditions, so important in determining the success or demise of the product & service behind the campaign.

In Japan, the manner in which space is organized and allocated is extremely original and efficient. Thirty-five square-metered apartments are quite common and integrally used up to the last remaining available spot. The bedroom, exhibiting the traditional Tatamis (rice straw mats), doubles as a living and as a sitting room. There are no double-panelled windows; there is no oven in the kitchen, reduced to a small inlaid kitchenette equipped with a gas stove below two electrical heating plates. The air conditioning is a mobile unit, serving both bed/living/sitting-room and bathroom, a small division with a bathtub, instead of a shower, so that it can hold the same water for a few days, which will be used in a variety of baths, re-heated, if necessary, by a gas-fuelled heater. Such lifestyle, totally different from that observed in

Europe or in the US will, for certain categories of products and services, necessarily require communication campaigns that are radically different from those produced in Europe or in the US - and advertising agencies are, or should be, aware of that.

Advertising draws from a variety of elements, one of them – an important one, if not the most important – the culture of the country or region in which the campaign is to be deployed. Although the world has become a global social web, sometimes it may be wise to differentiate strategies and communication campaigns at a local level.

Coca-Cola sells the same products with the same packaging and uses the same positioning and distribution strategies across the globe. However, the company often chooses to design promotional campaigns that are slightly different, depending on the location where it is being rolled-out. Coca-cola is therefore often referred to as having a multilocal strategy in what concerns promotion and advertising, conveniently adapted to local markets.

In 1998, the multilocal TV channel MTV tried to regain share in the Asian market by launching a 24-hour service with different musical line-ups and different shows being aired for different countries, careful enough not to hurt or offend local sensibilities, but bold enough not to give up its young, radical, hip and clashing image, a trademark of the channel, much appreciated by its target audiences.

Levi's Strauss is another multinational company following multilocal promotional guidelines, deploying local marketing strategies that differ according to the continent in which they are launched – Europe or US - and producing different advertising campaigns for each region. This geographic differentiation is motivated by the different positioning strategies the company chooses to adopt in each region: whilst in Europe, the brand Levi's exhibits premium price levels, thus appealing to a target with higher purchasing power, in the US prices are kept low, broadening the customer base.

Global vs. local campaign

Before deciding between a globally aligned campaign or a local focused promotion, it is of the utmost importance that advertisers fully understand the social and cultural traits of the markets in which they are operating, otherwise serious mistakes can be made, often leading to remarkable outcomes ranging from the withdrawal of the campaign to a public retraction or even apology, with an extremely negative impact on brand value and reputation, and, ultimately, on sales. But although this seems obvious enough, the fact remains that even the most prestigious and reputed companies, can be shown to have been less attentive in a not some distant past. Let's look at some examples:

Although Finland had committed to liberalize the advertising of alcoholic beverages since adhering to the EU in January 1995, its national authorities banned McCann Ericksson's Martini ad; the Finnish Ministry of Health and Social Affairs considered the spot to be excessive, with sexual connotations associated to alcohol that hurt the sensibilities of Finnish audiences. The short film depicted a mysterious well-dressed handsome man, wearing dark glasses, who offered a glass of Martini to a young blond accompanying a middle-aged millionaire. Seduced by the Martini Man, the blond beauty abandons her escort and walks away. Her tightly knit dress, however, gets caught in the chair where she was sitting, and, as she leaves, the dress starts to disappear, showing her beautiful model legs, thighs and lower buttocks. The censorship to the ad fuelled an enormous discussion in the media, with

Finnish government maintaining their position on the oversexualization of the female image and of alcohol, and Giovanni Parosino's Martini Rossi arguing for the adequacy and innocence of the advertising spot.

Sports brand Nike had to withdraw a sneaker model from the market due to cultural and religious pressures. While attempting to create an original design for the Nike Air shoes, the company came up with the idea of taking the word Air and shaping the letters so that they resembled the written name of the Muslim prophet Allah (Alá), a gesture that echoed negatively within the American-Muslim Council. Nike proceeded withdrawing of all the shoes from the market and presented a public apology to the Islamic community.

Publicis/London's "Firebird" advertisement for Publicis/Russia to promote Coca-Cola was developed around the concept of Russian legends. Its roll-out, however, was ill-received by the Russian community, considered it made a mockery of their cultural heritage, considered to have an almost sacred status amongst the Russian people.

It is also rather important, not to say absolutely indispensible, to have an efficient strategic plan to support the advertising campaign. When choosing a local strategy, it is imperative to pay attention to every historical, cultural, sociological and functional details. Spelling errors need to be avoided at all costs – and it is surprising how much they are not – the use of historic images or characters must also be refrained, and great care must be placed upon resorting to proverbs or traditional/popular expressions, to local iconography, to religious motives or even to historical or political facts, which need to be exact and precise. Again, what seems to be so straightforward and simple is sometimes easily forgotten. In a Peugeot campaign launched in the UK to promote the 106 "Inca" and the 205 "Azteca" models, the Inca version had the unfortunate slogan "Mexican's favourite", which immediately received an angry protest from London's Peruvian embassy. As a result, Peugeot rapidly presented his apologies to the Peruvian representatives and proceeded to immediately withdraw the ad.

CHAPTER 7

COMMUNICATION STRATEGIES AND PRODUCT LIFECYCLE

The end of the 19th century brought forth a number of brands that became known all over the world and still constitute, to this day, a huge success in sales. In 1863 two Americans came up with Royal powder, to be used by housewives to prepare desserts. Toblerone chocolate bars made their début in 1868, in Switzerland, and in 1886, John Pemberton, a pharmacist from Atlanta, US, sold bottles containing a brown syrup named Coca-Cola, only to be followed by Caleb Bradham, who launched the first Pepsi-Cola bottle twelve years later in North Carolina.

To certain experts, lasting products are those that have been able to address – and fill - vacant market niches, for exhibiting superior quality, widely acknowledged, and for having acquired an image that may easily be traced to cultural or traditional aspects of a certain region, country or even of an entire continent. For a brand to survive for several decades, other factors must also be in play, such as those indicated below:

Nature of the product: Some products are of such nature that remain virtually unaffected by changes, innovations or advances in technology. Such is the case of wine and spirits, milk, olive oil, deli products, cheese, and other goods that use specific traditional manufacturing processes – also called old fashioned, even though considerable technology may be present in their processing;

Attitude and Behaviour of the manufacturing, distributing and parent brand company: Not only towards its customers but also with respect to its stakeholders as well as the media;

Satisfaction of needs: Some products are able to satisfy needs that go beyond sensorial, functional or geographic motivations, as explained by Athaíde Marques in Mercator. For the consumer, the symbolism contained within and convened by the product may become a decisive factor that determines a purchase. Such is the case of Swatch watches, used symbolically as a fashion statement.

Modernization: Product lifecycle management

strategies rely on the smooth and progressive alteration of its quality, characteristics, performance, design and packaging, in a concerted and coherent effort to modernize its image and adapt it to the passing times. A product must always satisfy a need.

The brand must constantly pay attention to what the consumer wants, communicating reliability, confidence and trust on the product and nurturing the affectionate relationship between both. Age confers prestige; it transmits credibility, knowledge, experience, contributing to a deepening of the relationship between customer and product, which will tend to last longer.

According to Philip Kotler and Gary Amstrong (1998) in their book "Principles of Marketing" a product's lifecycle can be divided into four distinct stages:

Introduction: when the product is launched in the market, and sales growth is slow;

Growth: when there is an explosion in demand, a growth in revenues and profit and the product tends to become massified, with incumbents rising in an attempt to capture market share;

Maturity: when sales growth becomes slower; in this

stage, brands tend to embark in advertising and/or price wars;

Decline: Demand starts to slip, profits are rapidly eroded and the majority of competitors exit the market.

The hero is the customer, not the goods

Lester Wunderman, in his work, *"Being Direct, Making Advertising Pays"* (1996), states that it is the consumer, and not the product or service, that should be treated as a hero. The product or service must create value for each customer and satisfy his or her unique needs. Communication of the product or service must be clear and easily understandable and become as relevant and important to each single individual as the product or service itself, so that the customer may never feel compelled to ask, "why should I buy this product or service?"

Advertising should alter behaviours, not only (perceived) attitudes. The impact of advertising should be conveniently measured and evaluated in terms of return on investment. Customers must know the brand and think of it as an experience, serving their individual needs.

Fred Wiersema, in his book entitled "Customer Intimacy" (1998), argues that intimacy between customer and product, or service, is fundamental to create lasting relationships between buyer and brand. In fact, intimacy can only be created and maintained if the product, or service, possesses an actual use for the customer who purchases it. Upon making a purchase, the customer will not only acquire the product, or service, he or she will also buy its inherent and related benefits. The opinion made over the main benefits will 'close the deal', as it will determine the usefulness of the product or service and potentially motivate a repeat purchase.

In the book *"Focus, The Future of Your Company Depends on It"*, Al Ries (1996) maintains that the perception of quality of a product or service relies on four criteria. The first is the specialist effect: in the same way that a patient will prefer to consult a specialist over a general practitioner, whenever the suspicion of a serious illness or condition arises, so will the customer prefer a specialist's opinion to any other, and the more reputed the specialist, the highest his opinion will weigh. The second criterion is the leadership effect, whereupon consumers believe the product that sells the most is the best available; as such, communicating the market leadership position is a frequent move by brand owners (sometimes, regrettably, without any fundament). The third is the price effect: the higher the price, the greater the perception of quality and reliability. Finally, the fourth criterion is the brand reputation, which can impart benefits to the product, drawn from other products or services sold under the same brand name.

CHAPTER 8

EXPERT OPINIONS

Stan Rapp and Thomas Collins, in *"The New Maxi Marketing"* (1994), concluded that is fundamental to adopt a posture of communication, instead of one explicitly encouraging sales. An advertisement that attempts to push customers into making a purchase will be disregarded and easily forgotten. The customer wants to be given the information that will enable him to reach a decision without being pressured; and will have as high a consideration for a brand's image as the more benefits the promotional campaign will announce with the less explicit intention or concern regarding hard selling.

Rapp & Collins suggest the following guidelines to be taken into consideration upon designing a communication strategy:

Do not sell, communicate. The multiplicity of existing advertisements has crowded the customer's mind, causing a profound lack of interest over spots that push products or services. Tired of 'being sold things', the customer prefers to make his own decisions, in his own time...and with the information available, which must be communicated by the campaign(s).

Offer real benefits. It is best for the company's image and reputation to act before its customers than to simply talk. If a reliable, trustworthy bond is not created between customer and company, the former will hardly buy the latter's products or services.

Offer the consumer more for the same price. Customers want good value for their money, and demand quality and service. Small, unexpected, 'little extras' may be enough to justify charging higher prices than competitors.

Promote the interaction between customers and the organization. The company should stimulate customers to participate in joint events, programmes, clubs and so forth, nurturing the relationship between parties and fostering trust, intimacy and loyalty.

Jack Trout, states in *"The New Positioning"* (1996), that the last marketing battle is held inside the consumer's mind, which is insecure, confused in the variety of messages it receives, unable to process a multiplicity of stimuli and that also possesses a tendency to wander, whenever responding to a large number of requests. A sound communication campaign may use a series of instruments to enable a positive outcome, drawing to a successful close – the purchase. How? Well, first, the campaign must nudge the customer's emotions, For instance, it is wiser to depict a baby sleeping soundly and peacefully inside a car equipped with brand X tires, than to simply show the tire. Appealing to personal experiences, such as the birth of a child, a wedding anniversary or coming home from a tiring day at the office can also result in capturing the customer's attention.

Simplicity is the second instrument. A mobile phone that is too complex to use or possessing numerous and difficult to memorize functions may not sell well. Confusing concepts are also usually rejected: a vitamined deodorant, for instance, although combining popular and demanded features, will only generate confusion in the minds of consumers, since the benefits provided are not perceptually understood as a combined offer. Some of the most powerful concepts are based on a single word; one such example is that of Swedish carmaker Volvo, which the only value it conveys is safety

Acquired positioning is usually hard to alter. Coca-Cola, for instance, could not get a favourable reaction to the launch of the New Cola, which eventually was withdrawn from the market, while Volkswagen, so successful with its *beetle* model, could not convince American customers that it could manufacture big and fast cars. It is not uncommon that companies incur in serious positioning errors, especially upon launching new products / extensions lines. In today's fast-moving world, common advertising 'how-tos' and 'recipes' are becoming less effective and new advertising tools and supporting media are making their début.

Reality shows are an example of this. Depicting the daily lives of people has become a successful endeavour, with audiences tuning in to watch the latest developments in the lives of participants entering a competition or simply performing their daily tasks. Product placement and promotion in shows such as *Big Brother* or *Survivor* has been proven as an effective strategy. Another example can be made of TV series centered on strange phenomena, on the unknown. Such is the case of *The X-Files*, which has gathered followers around the world. Product placement in hit series is not new, but the show's format, duration and airing schedules may constitute a challenge for advertisers wishing to explore these supports and serve as *leit-motifs* for creating advertising pieces using similar concepts and trends.

CHAPTER 9

ADVERTISING MEDIA

The range and variety of existing and upcoming advertising media is wide, and advertisers must proceed carefully when defining the promotional strategy pertaining to a certain product or service, in order to choose, among the available supports, the most consistent and the most effective.

Printed Press

Some experts argue that the printed press still convey the most complete and detailed information among all media.

Pros: Printed press efficiently focuses the reader's attention, enhancing the exposure to its contents, and can be used as an information vehicle. It also allows for direct contact with audiences – through inserts, RSVP leaflets, or coupons (providing a wide range of coverage with great flexibility), possibility for segmentation at many levels (geographic, social, cultural, economic, professional, age, gender), variety of formats and distribution / promotional strategies. It also enables immediate product identification, using images with high resolution and appropriate colour palettes, and require flexible and affordable budgets, depending on the intensity and duration of the campaign.

Cons: Low coverage rates, especially in some segments and high costs per contact, especially if repeated. Also, the diversified audience requires varied supports.

Radio

Radio is an underestimated media, in terms of advertising, despite being very efficient in promoting recall and reaching audiences on a regular basis.

Pros: It fosters regular contacts with high repetition rates, enabling the possibility for target segmentation at various levels, such as age, gender and geography, as an example, with low cost per contact. Radio broadcast is an excellent means for obtaining a direct line to audiences, allowing feedback and interaction with its listeners; besides possessing relatively low production costs and short production times, radio is a privileged media support to launch tailored slogans and jingles that will promote rapid and lasting associations with the product, fostering awareness and stimulating recall.

Cons: Low coverage rates, for local broadcasts, inability to show and/or demonstrate the product and its features to the audience, rapid saturation due to the high levels of repetition.

Outdoor

The advertising message must be adjusted and adapted to the right formats: a static, large-scale image that will be displayed for a relatively short period of time. The lettering size must be adequate to passers-by and the message must be short and direct, and lengthy statements cannot be included. Any placed text must be read and understood at first glance by audiences who are often doing other tasks, such as driving, talking on the phone, walking the dog, watching their children, talking with friends, or thinking about the best possible route that will take them to their final destination.

In the 90's, the outdoor was Benetton's chosen advertising support for its advertising campaigns. Its unique, bold and borderline shocking campaigns depict both models and common people, with distinct unstereotyped features dressed in loud colours, have managed to grant the brand a frontline position in the fashion world. The use of nudes, amputees, religious icons or terminally ill patients in its advertising campaigns has fuelled Benetton's reputation as fresh, innovative and hip, which, in turn, has lead other media to often mention the brand and its achievements, thus increasing its awareness, with a consequent impact on sales.

Pros: Good penetration rates, since an outdoor is seen – even involuntarily – by each and every passer-by, with high levels of repetition. The outdoor if efficient in showing the product and promoting recall, with high cross-selling potential with other media supports, reinforcing brand awareness. It provides flexibility in terms of contact rate (in number of displays) and in the nature of the support used (billboards, spectacolor, rotating panels, banners, flags, urban furniture...).

Cons: Inadequate for conveying sophisticated advertising messages. Production-related technical requirements may demand high costs and long-term planning.

Direct Marketing

Content must be objective, otherwise audiences will be confused, bored or even annoyed, since they know that whenever a company takes the time to write directly at them, it usually means that company intends to sell something.

The advertising message must highlight aspects of the product or service, such as its reliability, or the satisfaction level of other customers who have bought the good, together with warranties against possible faults or damages incurred exclusivity of its distribution channels, limited availability or even well-known individuals that have purchased the product or service and highly recommend it. A good value proposition must supersede expectations, generate enthusiasm and encourage the purchase.

Creativity is also – and always – an added benefit; in 1996, TAP Air Portugal sent a mailing letter that made the sound of a plane taking off the runway whenever the letter was unfolded, which generated an enormous buzz and increased the company's awareness.

Direct Mail is, however, more than sending trinkets, offers, coupons or vouchers. It must possess the right tone and convey an appropriate message to the consumers it is sent to, in order to produce the expected outcome. For this to happen, it is fundamental that the advertising agency understands the preferences and habits of the targeted segments and express them, simply and clearly, in the written message.

Writing a winning message is never an easy task. A known marketing specialist published an article defining a few simple guidelines to structure both content and form of a direct mail advertising message: useless sentences and words must be suppressed; sentences should not exceed a maximum of 10 or 15 words; vocabulary should be kept simple; passive and future verbal forms should be replaced by present and imperative cases; indefinite notions must be replaced, made objective and precise; action verbs must be used. Also to be avoided is a straightforward and unjustified familiarity with the audience, together with an impersonal treatment, ill-placed humour, comples word games, highly intellectualized messages or technical terms.

It is unwise to treat the customer as a mere revenue-generating instrument, forgetting the "real person". Advertisers must be reminded at all times that people enjoy being surprised and taken care of, instead of being viewed as mere vehicles that will enable the fulfilment of sales objectives. Customers want to be thrilled and excited; they need to feel joyful, optimistic or even passionate about the product to the point of there being no other alternative than its purchase. As such, companies should take great care in creating strong bonds and nurturing the relationship with their customers, instead of simply attempting at generating impact with their advertising campaigns.

Reactions to direct marketing can be both direct and indirect. In any case, they are of the utmost importance for the companies promoting their brands, as consumer reactions are no less than the responses to the advertising campaign they have designed, playing an important role in helping to understand the real motivations behind the success – or demise – of the campaign and enabling action to be taken in order to correct any found mistakes or reinforce the positive strategies.

Each cent invested in advertising should have a positive impact on the company's bottom-line profit, and direct marketing is a reliable way of achieving this. If carefully planned and executed, its results can be measured and the return on investment calculated, which constitute a meaningful advantage with respect to other advertising media. Direct marketing allows for straightforward measuring of the outcome of an advertising campaign, with the added advantage of allowing companies to build customer – even if potential ones – databases, which can later be used in customer relationship management and loyalty programmes.

The categories most prone to be promoted via direct marketing during the eighties and the nineties were books, food products, beverages, clothing and household utilities. Today, this medium is used for a variety of products, services and even in corporate branding.

Some authors defend that loyalty was the obsession during the nineties. With products offering less and less competitive advantages, customer service and post-sale relationship management were (and still are) key to add value for the customer.

Direct marketing creates contact opportunities that must not be wasted with ill-conceived messages or strategies. Text must be carefully structured, with the product's main benefit highlighted in the first paragraph - the value drawn by the customer, explicitly stated and examples or samples, including claims duly supported by testimonials from previous users. It is also important to let the receiver know what will be forfeited if he/she will not respond promptly, and therefore being encouraged by the usage of further incentives explained in the letter.

Pros: Selectivity, since it allows for a careful selection of the target audience; personalization, by using the recipient's name and address; recall, since an intelligently structured and produced mailing will remain in the audience's memory; versatility, for it is relatively easy to send any type of object with any sort of format via mail; lasting, since direct mailing is something tangible that can remain at reach for specific period of time; ease to reply, if including an RSVP coupon or envelope or even a direct telephone number or an email address; measurable, since it originates direct replies that allow a better understanding of the campaign's strengths and weaknesses, as well as its return; perfectible, in the sense that it provides feedback for posterior improvements; adjustable, as it allows for a series of test runs to be made before a wider distribution, enabling minor corrections.

Cons: Medium to long term planning due to production constraints of technical nature and database mining – these can limit the number of targets to contact and the non-existence, or lack of characterization of some segments (data) in most databases.

Television

The number of TV sets in Portugal is estimated to be much larger than the number of refrigerators; as such, Portugal was, during the 90's, a country where TV was a much appreciated and widely used media to convey advertising campaigns. With the dawn of cable TV, the number of available channels has increased exponentially and, correspondingly, the number of possibilities for placing an ad. Brought to Portugal by TVCabo, cable allowed Portuguese audiences the access to information and services until then unavailable, granting advertisers multiple contact opportunities for launching promotion strategies. It also ensured a high signal-to-noise ratio; in other words, the quality of the TV signal delivered by cable was superior to airborne broadcasts, which fuelled the increase in the number of cable subscribers and therefore granted extremely high rates of penetration of cable television in Portuguese homes.

This broadening in terms of channel offering – TVCabo allowed access to 30 different channels, targeting viewers with different preferences – information, science, children programmes, movies, music and so forth, some of these (such as Panda, Hollywood, Odyssey, Sol or even Discovery) already had lined-up advertising campaigns targeting the interests of the consumer segments they aimed for. These new channels adapted to match language, culture and other local characteristics, in orderto provide an appropriate geographic broadcast segmentation.

Other products such as *Pay-per-view, teleshopping, and video on demand* or TV games have also experienced growth in terms of awareness and number of viewers/users.

In the case of teleshopping, products are shown and demonstrated on TV, and then made available to purchase to an audience via a landline (or more recently, using unline mechanisms) to which viewers can call, order the product, pay for it – if choosing to do so – and have the product conveniently delivered. Aired in Portugal for the first time in 1993, teleshopping is currently available in several channels, both national and international.

To successfully telemarket a product, this needs to possess innovative features and also be unavailable everywhere else except on TV – to add to these requirements, the product should also be solely available for the duration of the promotional spot (or for a few minutes after). It is also necessary that viewers be segmented in terms of airing schedules in order to select the most adequate product portfolio to present and the most favourable schedule. For instance, housewives are TV viewers during mornings and early afternoons. Household products, such as pots, pans, dining sets and kitchen utensils are products most sought for and directed at this segment.

Pros: TV is a media with great impact, allowing for high levels of quality and penetration in the majority – if not all – segments. It possesses a wide (national as well as international) coverage, with flexibility in the choice of schedule, duration, type of programmes associated with or leading/trailing the ad, promotion strategy (showcase, full-length demonstration, featured appearance, endorsement, sponsorship, contests, teleshopping, games, telethons, just to name a few) and low cost per contact.

Cons: Advertising saturation, long-term planning, high production costs, short lifespan, audience fragmentation, dispersed by a higher number of available channels andreduced shares.

Cinema

Advertisers are returning to movie theatres. As advertising pollution crowds TV channels, challenging its value and efficacy as a reliable information, education and entertainment support, companies have turned to theatres, newly renewed, with state of the art audio and visual technology as an alternative for promoting their products or services.

A study, conducted in Denmark, aiming at understanding how the cinema scene relates and impacts on both the advertisement and the advertised good. It has concluded that viewers consider watching the advertising piece and the film as a complete and integrated experience of going to the movies. As such, the quality experience drawn from watching the film is broadened and shared with products being advertised, which obviously increases the products' perceived value to the viewer. The study also mentions that running costs depend on the movie being shown and, in some cases, the day of the week it is screened.

In Portugal, in the late nineties, there was still not enough information available on this media. Still, comparisons can be drawn with other media, particularly with its 'kindred-media' television. As such, from an investment perspective, and with respect to the cost per contact, it is more expensive to advertise in cinema than in television; however, cinema provides a qualitatively different experience, with safe and reliable touching points and with captive audiences, as Reis (1997) rightfully states, "with the particular feature of never becoming excessive, of not tiring or annoying audiences". The author also indicates that products or services targeting younger audiences are beginning to rely on cinema as an expressive support, with particular relevance for automobiles, food and beverages, banking and telecommunications. Goods targeting housewives are usually not good candidates for this media.

For the campaign to be successful, it is necessary that the advertising film has a good plot or story behind, an appropriately mood-setting soundtrack and a superior technical quality. After all it will always be compared with the ensuing film. As such, it is not unusual that movie directors and producers are hired by advertising companies to make the advertising piece targeted to theatres, often choosing film instead of video recording, for added quality.

Cinema allows for an efficient segmentation of the target audience due to its intrinsic characteristics such as seasonality, with the so-called 'back to school' period occurring in the last trimester of each year. Also, and according to market research data pertaining to the first semester of the year 1996 in Portugal, a study performed by Marktest, the towns of Lisbon and Oporto together make up for more than half of the country's moviegoers during that period, with movie premieres peaking in affluence.

In order to best typify and characterize cinema audiences with reliable and regular data, the Portuguese Institute for Cinema and Audiovisuals, IPACA, has brought forward a most ambitious project aiming at setting up a computerized information system connecting every theatre's ticket office to a central database, shared by movie distributors and exhibitors, and accessible to other information media.

Pros: The audience's perception and expectations towards the featured film increases the value of the advertising displayed, promoting secure and credible contacts, directed at varied audiences.

Cons: Higher production and placement costs, number

of contacts depending on the movie's share of audience, reduced attention span from viewers arriving late to the theatre.

Internet

This is a media with growing importance due to the rising and swift penetration of New Media worldwide. During the first trimester of 1998 the sum of US$351M has been invested in internet advertising, 27% of which in computer products and services, 25% in general consumption goods, 13% in financial services and 10% in New Media related goods, according to the Internet Advising Bureau.

Throughout its eleven years of existence, American rock band *Widespread Panic* has never had a video clip featured in MTV, nor had any of its songs ever reached the top 200 in *Billboard* Magazine. Still, the band managed to gather quite a legion of fans having even afforded the luxury to refuse opening a *Rolling* Stones concert tour. In 1998, the band gathered a record of 100,000 fans in Athens, Georgia, transforming this into one of the most successful CD launches in history. "Madonna or Elton John can manage that, but few others performers do", stated Edgar Neiss, Fox General Manager in Atlanta, GA.

The band's success clearly illustrates the grassroots and viral marketing potential of the internet, used by fans, youngsters with ages ranging from 25 to 30 years old, daily surfing the web for the latest news regarding their favourite performers, for having the opportunity to make direct contact with *Panic* band members via the purposefully created *Widespread Panic* webpage, and know their preferences such as what they have had for lunch on a specific day or even what were their favourite movies of all times. The band's manager confirmed that the traffic increase on the group's webpage – designed and set-up by a fan – helped raise record sales from US$100K in 1996 to US$350K in 1998.

The Internet has become a media type preferred by consumers as well as companies and advertisers, as a mean to massively promote products and services. The use of a banner is probably the most common way of advertising in the web, usually rectangular in shape and featuring the product's characteristics and benefits. Its cost is based on the number of prints or visualizations, which can be tracked and audited by external specialists.

In Portugal during the nineties, profiling website audiences was limited to tracking the site's number of visits, which was considered to be enough to justify pricing schedules of advertising space. Some companies, however, would take the number of downloads performed on the site for number of visits to that site while others considered the number of WebPages visited within the site as actual number of visits to the website, which obviously inflated counters.

Other barriers were found by companies wishing to advertise on the web, such as being unable to count and profile viewers of ads placed in external sites, to which companies had limited or no access to.

In order to address data gathering and mining from web users, companies like Initiative Media have launched specific software to enable the collection of information from web surfers, in an attempt to allure advertisers to use this new media.

Planning an advertising campaign to be screened only by certain website users (target audience) in certain locations in the world is nowadays trivial. This enables efficient and effective target segmentation and a corresponding customization of the advertising piece.

Potential customers are only a mouse click away from an advertiser's webpage, and advertisers know it. They can collect feedback over their products or obtain valuable information regarding their customers, existing or potential. As such, advertising, customer relations and sales end up virtually joined together, almost indistinguishable in cyberspace.

In the US and in many European countries, there are companies specializing in selling or facilitating the sale of advertising space on the web. When managing advertising space for several websites, companies usually tend to sell entire pages or blocks of space within a page, allowing advertisers to audit and control web traffic and content within that space. Websites also try single-handedly to sell advertising space on their own site.

When the Internet first arrived to Portugal, sales of advertising space were disappointing, with more banners claiming, "Advertise here" than actual sales. Yet, in 1999, a large number of individuals requested internet access from service providers, mainly students, scientists and businesspeople, and forecasts estimated a exponential growth in the number of users for the subsquent years, together with an expansion of this media to other segments of the population. Currently, children start surfing the web at the age of 10 – some even before. These are the so-called "customers of the future".

In the US, the internet is much more disseminated. In 1996 the advertising investment amounted to €200M, while outside the US, the value paled to a mere €5M, according to Jupiter Communications.

Pros: The advantages of this media are many; the interactivity provided, the large amount of information that can be made available at the click on a banner, the lack of a time limit or schedules for visualizing the ad, the possibility for accurate target segmentation and the possibility of gathering reliable and precise data regarding user profiles and origin, as well as advert visibility, attractiveness and return on investment. It also allows for other media and event coverage (free advertising) as well as content customization, allowing companies to foster one-to-one relationships with final consumers and to launch new products, product line extensions or new advertising campaigns to existing products, tailored to customers' preferences.

Cons: In the 90's, it had relatively low penetration rates, very restricted to middle to upper-middle social strata. The internet is a media requiring advertisers to master new technologies and respective stakeholders in order to take full advantage of its capabilities.

CHAPTER 10

ADVERTISING PLACEMENT

Planning an advertising campaign requires a clear definition of the goal to achieve as well as the market segment to target. It then becomes necessary to manage the campaign budget so that objectives are reached within the required timeframes.

With only a limited number of TV channels available in Portugal in the 80's and 90's – two, controlled by government-appointed managers - managing them was a relatively easy task; with the entrance of incumbents such as privately owned channels, together with satellite and cable channels, TV advertising became a highly specialized ordeal.

Price schedules for TV spots vary according to channel and are proportional to ratings. A less expensive alternative for advertising on TV consists in placing the brand in a specific show, usually displaying a brief slide immediately before or after the programme, even in breaks. This constitutes an interesting strategy, for granting prestige to the brand by association with the show whilst allowing an efficient segmentation.

Television Series

Together with soap operas, TV series are the programmes that rate higher in audiences, with a large span in age, from youngsters to elderly viewers. Family themes, everyday life situations, humour and comedy shows are among themes that have higher success in terms of audience. These audiences have the tendency to put themselves in the shoes of TV characters, a fact that network managers keep in mind when producing or purchasing shows for broadcast. Together with the cast, the intended airing schedule and, obviously, the cost associated, factors such as the quality of the series and its pertinence are carefully evaluated when a purchase decision is to be made.

Successful TV series are often relegated to late hour schedules, in an attempt to hold audiences captive for longer periods of time - this leads to an increase of available and profitable advertising schedules. In Europe and in North America, primetime is usually set between 8.00 pm to 11.00 p.m., and it is then that the most popular shows are aired, with the greater audiences.

Although there is no winning recipe for a TV series to become successful, a series of guidelines should be respected in order to win audiences over. Amongst them:

A good script, depicting daily situations to which viewers can easily relate to, becoming more attentive and interested in further episodes;

Happy endings, capable of inducing good feelings that allow viewers to forget their own troubles and life ordeals. Sensitive matters or subjects that may hurt or offend viewers' sensibilities must, at all costs, be avoided or properly packaged;

Subject matters including melodramatic elements, touching serious aspects of viewers' lives, bearing some sort of social impact, or pertaining to specific professional groups;

Stories that may be easily apprehended and comprehended by all family elements;

Natural succession of events, so the viewer can follow the plot easily, without getting lost in details;

The more famous the cast, the more audiences the series draws;

Closed narrative episodes, with a clear beginning, middle and end, to grant closure to audiences;

Simple dialogues, direct enough so as not to cause confusion or raise questions; characters and set should also be easily identifiable;

Use of references to the Unknown. All things connected with the 'mysterious universe of the unknown' exert great attraction over audiences. Aliens, space wars, paranormal phenomena and transcendental episodes have been explored by networks as a means for increasing ratings. One such example is the series *'X-Files'*, a worldwide success dabbling on the borders of reality.

In 1999 television line-ups were held hostages of ratings, which evidenced the commercial nature of broadcasts – including state-owned channels – that demanded advertising revenues to ensure their sustainability. High ratings came with sensationalism, with less care for keeping viewers reliably informed than for bombarding them with appellative, eye-opening shows with little context or content. In truth, viewers do not want to be delivered straightforward news; they prefer stories, the more emotional the better.

This conclusion drawn from statistical data pertaining to information on audiences of certain shows legitimates network managers to subvert both criteria for selecting which news to present as well as the manner in which this information is presented to viewers; in other words, which stories are told and the manner in which they are relayed.

Yves Eudes, reporter from French newspaper Le Monde and TV producer, takes from his research on US media to suggest that information programmes have become entertaining shows, carefully planned to captivate audiences and make money. TV networks use techniques such as interrupting programmes with 'last minute' shocking news or events, or the inclusion of advertising blocks immediately before and during breaks in news broadcasts.

In his opinion, the use of such techniques, together with the growing trend for news anchors to use words and expressions more suited to game shows and entertainment programmes have regretfully transformed news shows into action features.

Interactive TV

When interactive television was launched, an enormous revolution took place in the household electronics industry. With numerous opportunities to be explored, this media has several applications, which will tend to maintain viewers captive. Amongst these, the following must be mentioned:

Leisure: Access to *entertainment on demand*, possibility of ordering, electronically, a specific show, series episode, *video-on-demand*; games or other entertainment programmes or even applications (also called - apps);

Family Management: *Teleshopping*, banking services, videophone, e-mail access, and other services available, such as electronic reservations of restaurants, hotels and theatre tickets;

Education: Facilitate access to online education, learning programmes and cultural programmes

Companies: Videoconference communications, access to databases and portable filing systems, electronic offices and long distance training & certification.

It is exciting to think about the wonders interactive television can provide. Using only a keyboard, it is possible to surf the web using a TV set, a reality that will certainly and seriously influence advertisers behaviours and communication strategies.

CHAPTER 11

SATURATION:
THE EXCESS OF ADVERTISING

It is still unknown whether the interruption of films and TV programmes for the purpose of running advertisements is appreciated and valued by the consumer, as it is not fully understood the possible returns generated by this procedure.

The seemingly apparent spontaneity of an avalanche of promotional pieces during a commercial break is everything but random. The fact that toys are advertised during early morning children TV shows, or that tyres, motor oils and cars are shown during the broadcast of F1 trials and events are proof that advertisement line-ups are carefully planned according to expected viewing segments.

With the appearance of privately-held TV networks and channels, advertising became a much more specialized activity, where, besides considering the placement of a piece from a price vs. ratings perspective, new opportunities and new ideas could be articulated with imagination to best design campaigns that may suit the target under consideration whilst taking advantage of the network line-up.

According to Tavares & Bustorff (1997), consumers attitudes regarding advertising messages is extremely variable, depending on the age, gender as well as on the social, economical, cultural and educational characteristics of each individual, as well as the message's content and nature. In the specific case of promotional blocks inserted in TV programmes, the authors maintain that consumers will tend to view adverts attentively and retain the main message provided that it is aligned with the show's theme.

Common to the majority of human beings, we all tend, at some point, to listen without hearing, to watch without seeing or even to read without fully comprehending the whole text. Information anxiety is a state of mind driven by the distress a person feels when believing not to be grasping the full concept; when sensing a tangible distance from what is learned and what should have been perceived.

In the "The Micro Revolution Revisited", Peter Large states that the amount of information generated in the last century is equal to that produced in the preceding five thousand years. Every day, around one thousand new book titles see the dawn, while the written output tend to double every eight years. Communication media seeks to offer the largest amount of information within the shortest time possible; everyday we are harassed by worldwide events and issues in a number impossible to be duly assimilated and the more we seek to keep ourselves informed, the more we incur in perception and assimilation errors or even in developing information anxiety 'symptoms'. The more one seeks to invest in learning about multiple distinct events, the less one manages to understand the reasons and the motivations behind the facts, to observe patterns and connections between apparently unrelated actions and attitudes, to duly contextualize history. Instead, we prefer being put to rest by a mind-numbing flow of endlessly shallow information and unsubstantiated data, offering nothing but a fleeting and often twisted glimpse of reality.

To William Davis and Allison McCormack in "*The Information Age*", facts need to be supported by data and it is the reasoning that comes from piecing the facts together that is perceived as information. Random and unconnected data possess little meaning unless grouped and duly processed. As such, excessive communication may result in absence of meaning, in excess of trivial data, in saturation. The ineffable Don Juan would say, 'the more time spent in seducing a woman, the less the disposition to love her". The same happens with information, where the more, the less.

The excess of advertising is a quantifiable phenomenon. According to Orrin Klapp in his book *"Overload and Boredom: Essays on the Quality of Life in the Information Society"* (1986), boredom may result from lack of information as much as it may be caused by excessive stimulation. In fact, excess of information frequently degenerates in noise, redundancy, banality, as information is delivered at a much faster pace than it is fully absorbed and apprehended. If advertising constitutes an indispensible driver for the purchase of products and services, the excess of advertising has the exact opposite effect, with even the most imaginative, bold and disruptive pieces going unnoticed by audiences.

An example is found in Tokyo, where the impact of advertising is enormous; each available surface is overloaded with advertising messages, in all sorts of advertising supports, be them static, dynamic, interactive, multi-dimensional, colourful, with many formats, running day and night. People simply do not pay attention. But the blame is not confined to the busy Japanese capital, as we too, are sinners. We are all accustomed to TV ads, being aired during commercial breaks, often preceded by an announcement indicating its start and followed by another marking its end. Those who have never channel surfed or paid short visits to the bathroom or simply wandered away from the TV set during promotional breaks should now speak or forever hold their silence!.

Is it possible, then, to bypass the excess in advertising? Well, the answer is yes, if performed in an intelligent and clever manner. Both advertising agencies and companies have been working in addressing simple, original ways of increasing brand awareness, by devising effective communication strategies. One such example is engaging in dissimulated advertising. Companies are investing in the film industry as a means of penetrating into the minds of consumers in a non-intrusive manner. Apple, for instance, has disbursed US$2.5M to have its products features in blockbuster hit *"Mission Impossible"*. Product placement also occurs in other media, and in other formats, as noted below.

Brazilian comedian Jô Soares relied on his IBM laptop, conveniently – and visibly - placed upon his "Jô Soares Onze e Meia" hosting table to aid him throughout his talk-show interviews;

BMW convinces James Bond to trade in his fashionable Aston Martin for one of its most recent models, the BMW Z4, launched simultaneously with the movie, in a concerted massive marketing operation;

Brazilian soap opera *"Tieta do Agreste"* featured a scene where one of the main characters received a cashier's check from Brazil's Banco Real;

Coca-Cola planned on painting the Indianapolis in red and white stripes, its brand colours, as it is forbidden to advertise inside the facility;

Pizza Hut managed to insert its logo on the pizzas ordered by the Teenage Mutant Ninja Turtles in the Videogame developed for PlayStation.

The Red Stripe beer was an unknown brand in the US, until Tom Cruise opened the fridge and took out a bottle, in the movie *"The Firm"*. From then on, the product achieved immediate recognition and sales more than justified the US$5M invested by the company in the manoeuvre.

These examples show that brands have moved from conventional media to more elaborated vehicles, in an attempt to surprise audiences in a dissimulated, but effective fashion, with added credibility. Whenever viewers watch a commercial, they are aware that the advertising message provides a unilateral, paid and often biased version of the product or service showcased; however, if a movie actor, a TV character, an opinion leader or an influencer is observed actually using the product or service, the consumer is more easily swayed into the purchase, and the brand is perceived with added credibility, resulting in higher awareness and recall levels.

Industries view movies as an opportunity to launch trends, with brands attempting to enact carefully dissimulated penetration strategies within movie scripts. But not all succeed. In a research performed by the McCollum Spelman Institute, more than one third of the almost 5,000 scrutinized films failed to foster recall and promote persuasion.

CHAPTER 12

MARKET RESEARCH

As soon as Telecel (actual Vodafone) started operating in Portugal, incumbent TMN began treading the painful road of market share loss and brand awareness decrease, which generated conflicts within the company. To overcome this unfavourable context, TMN tried to gain further knowledge in understanding its customer's true needs and engaged in a market research that would allow this brand to support the conception and implementation of a customer-focused strategy, together with an advertising campaign that would meet their target demands and enable market share recapture.. The study concluded that customers valued signal coverage and quality and often complained about customer service, which led TMN to set priorities that would enable the company to attain its goals.

First, it was necessary to implement changes at a technical level, acting on the product, which would exhibit higher overall quality parameters. Only then would customer service be addressed, as it would be unwise to invest in this front without the assurance, or, at least, the possibility of capturing new customers and segments. As a result, in 1994, the company decided to shift part of its advertisement budget to operations, only to launch new promotional campaigns when most technical issued had been addressed. The ensuing campaign addressed a new model, the *TMN Spot*, a pre-paid mobile phone using a small Ericsson device with high autonomy, targeting younger audiences. Upon purchasing a *Spot*, the customer would not immediately pay for its full value. Instead, the customer would be able to divide this amount into 12 small and comfortable instalments, payable via ATM, throughout the first year of use. Together with an attractive billing schedule and with reduced tariffs from Friday through Sundays, the product was an immediate hit with youngsters, who found the new product – with renewed technical characteristics - extremely attractive, giving a boost to the company's sales revenues.

This is just an example of how market research can provide information about the identification of problems and needs. Market research can also be used to test consumer reactions to a product or a service before its launch. It allows advertisers to probe which type of campaigns will have a better fit with specific target audiences, maximizing the willingness to purchase and repeat the purchase. Without a careful and dedicated investigation into consumer preferences, many mistakes can be made. Such is the case of US mattress company, Simmons & Co., which decided to invest a small fortune in an advertising campaign to launch its products in the Japanese market. Foregoing any market research, the company deployed its strategy, flooding Japan with plush, high quality mattresses, certain they would become a success in sales. The product was a flop. Why? Japanese sleep on Tatamis, thin and hard surfaces, usually laid on the floor...

There is a large amount of statistical information pertaining to and available to most countries that allow a fairly good understanding of the habits and major preferences of its targets. Companies such as Gartner and Nielsen conduct ongoing studies to provide reliable and current market-related data. In Portugal, every year a market research company named Marktest puts out a collection of statistical information to allow for a profiling of its residents, compiled in a book entitled *"General and Marketing Facts"*. Throughout the chapters included in the above mentioned book, namely macroeconomics, external trade, economic activity, private companies, population, social data, consumption and lifestyle, media and advertising, international and information guide, Marktest aims to provide answers to senior management and advisory boards to enable them to make appropriate decisions.

The current age of information is in fact defined by an explosion of facts, an avalanche of raw data, which need to be conveniently assimilated by individuals, in order to be valued. To Claude Shanon and Warren Weaver, in *"The Mathematical Theory of Communication"*, information is what reduces uncertainty. More often than not, consumers want things they cannot express in words nor, in some cases, in an intelligible manner. Reactions such as like/dislike/accept/do not accept/agree/do not agree and so forth obtained from market researchers, must be understood in light of the mechanism and underlying concepts pertaining to the situation under analysis.

A correct and well-planned market research study needs to be able to identify aspirations, fears, wants, desires and needs from apparently unrelated responses, carefully elaborated by experienced researchers, which will, in a later stage, be cautiously decoded and systematized. No one expects a person to start rambling about the depths, breadths and heights of emotions generated by eating a potato chip, or about the thrill of erotic feelings arousing from using a certain brand of perfume.

Upon being interviewed by researchers, people will

shun from being too eloquent and will tend to behave with composure and as rational as possible. Upon saying "I do nor agree" over a certain statement or advertising piece, a subject may simply be expressing a discomfort for being shown something unusual, to which he or she is not accustomed to, instead of simply manifesting a dislike. This also can be used by advertisers to their favour, especially if the concept behind the campaign shown is a breakup with current values and traditions.

Market research studies are, in sum, a useful tool to allow companies and advertisers to better understand their target segments, explore new markets, develop new products, line extensions or proceed to alter existing ones as well as to better assess risks. Research must be used as an instrument to enable a sound strategic planning, with focus and consistency, establishing priorities and enabling decisions, allowing advertisers to work with reliable guidelines and within a framework to produce unbarred and unrestrained creative pieces, with definable boundaries and outcomes.

JWT's Tavares & Bustorff (1997) have conducted a study to be used exclusively by advertisers and brands addressing people's attitudes towards the media. The methodology consisted on performing 1932 interviews, stratified by *habitat*, in locations with a population starting from 2 000 inhabitants, with ages from 15 to 50 years of age, in the cities of Lisbon and Oporto. Besides socio-demographic variables, the study also screened for different occasions during the day, behaviours & attitudes as well as for the type and theme of the programme that fostered the contact with the media under observation. Subjects were divided into four groups, according to their tendencies and attitude towards life. These groups were: conservative/routine, serious vs. non-impulsive, light vs. curious and pioneers vs. advanced. One major conclusion of the study was the ability to distinguish the subjects' attention level towards a programme based on their attitude & behaviour towards the respective support media.

According to the authors there is an enormous difference between people who have their TV sets turned on during the entire day and those who only flip the remote for a 15-minute period; while the former look at the TV set as something that will keep them company, the latter only resort to watching television when they actually want to, and during a short period in which they are watching a show. As such, it is important to decode ratings for what they really mean, instead of taking raw data by itself. In fact, it can be shown that some shows possessing smaller audiences are often viewed with more interest than record-beating soap operas and TV game shows, for instance. Furthermore, subjects often perform other activities such as reading, talking, cooking or cleaning while watching TV. The study showed that during a TV music show, 53% of pioneers/advanced subjects were paying undivided attention, while 28% ate and drank, 11.5% worked, 7% performed household duties and 5% chatted. Such type of information is crucial for a good media strategic planning.

Upon defining the target for a certain brand, a single 15 minutes insertion with undivided attention may be enough to promote recall.

In most countries there are companies specializing in TV programming, supplying qualitative and quantitative analysis of audiences with extreme detail and accuracy. One such example is "Telédia", which relates audience data with programme schedule and content, by the minute, 24/7. This enables a better understanding of rating variability by channel and per programme, allowing for the identification of strengths and weaknesses of line-ups as well as viewers reactions to certain contents. It also allows the spotting of certain behaviours: for instance, it has been shown that Portuguese viewers relentlessly surf the channels, clicking furiously on their remotes, whenever a commercial break is presented as well as during comedy shows or musical intermissions.

CHAPTER 13

ADVERTISING FESTIVALS AND AWARDS

Advertising festivals can be divided into two main types: one directed at creativity and the other rewarding effectiveness. Creativity awards aim at fostering inventiveness, originality and innovation, while effectiveness awards look at the actual results, in terms of awareness, recall and sales, generated by the campaign, with participants required to produce detailed reports with key data to corroborate their claims. Other festivals exist, in which a variety of features and characteristics, such as advertising techniques, comedy, reduced budgets and local advertising campaigns are assessed.

The evaluation criteria used to rank the different works presented vary from festival to festival, and, within the same festival, from category to category. Chosen amongst reputed advertising professionals, a jury may also bring on board clients, media experts as well as marketing, business development and sales specialists, individuals respected and recognized by the industry, conferring prestige and added credibility to the ceremony. Together with the quality of the presented pieces and the ensuing media coverage, the jury reputation will certainly add value to the event. Creativity is not an art form *per se*, but instead, a vehicle to aid clients in selling their products and services. As such, some experts tend to consider efficacy awards, such as UK's IPA awards, more important than those contemplating creativity.

Advertising events usually reward differentiation, originality, risk and creativity as success drivers. Receiving an award is a synonym, to an advertising agency, of increased drive, dynamics, quality, efficacy and perfectionism. Also, awards are true motivators to the creative teams responsible for design & campaign conception, serving as magnets for the recruitment of new talents or seasoned professionals by award-winning agencies as well as for new clients or brands looking for a new advertising agency, trusting that their brilliant trak record will also be used in their campaign.

It is not unusual for gold to be bestowed on the wildest, funniest, boldest, more intelligent ideas, or those farthest from current trends or conventions. Humour may also be a shoe-in, as it is simplicity equally understood by all countries, races and social strata. In some cases, there may even be no need for copy, easily inferred from the images depicted in the winning pieces, often exhibiting an extreme care in the choice of lighting, colours, image treatment and the many other visual elements, free from all the annoying and distressing visual and verbal pollution. Many of the pieces exhibited at festivals depict wonderful cases in which typical and everyday human reactions are intelligently used by creatives and successfully linked to brands, products and services.

For agencies to be able to devise impactful and innovative campaigns, there has to be a client bold enough to encourage and support its development and final approval.

In 1985/86 *Marketing & Publicidade*, a Portuguese magazine dwelling on marketing and advertising issues, conducted a series of interviews directed at known Portuguese advertisers and marketers, concluding that most advertising films would not be presented at the Cannes Festival, which privileged creativity and innovation in determent of effec*tiveness*. In their opinion, "The advertising pieces that actually sell the product have usually zero or close to zero creativity and/or entertainment, but are ripe in strategy and results". In Cannes we see the prettiest pieces, produced with extreme technical quality and concern for originality and innovation, but with strategy taking a back seat. As a result, sometimes they sell the product – as with the case of Levi's Strauss 1998 US campaigns - and other times – more often than not – they don't.

What would then be the true purpose of advertising festivals if award-winning adverts would be unable to sell the corresponding products or services? What will be the true value of an advertising campaign that cannot persuade consumers into making a purchase? It is not that hard to imagine the disappointment of a client who has approved an award-winning, widely acclaimed campaign that has had no success in terms of increasing sales or even product & service awareness.

In summary, advertising is not pure *show business*. It has a true purpose, a real attainable goal that of selling, in its gerenal meaning. More than ideas, it is imperative that other factors, such as commitment, talent, persuasion, ability to motivate and drive a purchase, to aid companies to increase revenues, to grow and expand their business; in other words, to bring together technical and functional effectiveness with oriented and focused creativity.

This approach doesn't always mean a considerable investment, or substancial time for conception and implementation to get things right. Every year at

Cannes, a seminar on low budget productions is held with surprising presentations. One such example are Swedish advertisements, taped using a simple, domestic-use video recorder, with astounding impact ... and often awarded!

CHAPTER 14

SUCCESS CASES
IN PORTUGUESE ADVERTISING

Banco Mello

The Portuguese banking sector was, until 1997, focused on aggressive hard-selling strategies, often using hermetic language and resorting to numbers, not fully understood by consumers, when conveying their advertising messages. Also humorous contents were often employed, not always in a successful manner, upon promoting financial products. Banco Mello, decided on a fresh approach. Opting for humanized messages, informative and educational in content, the bank tried to go against the mainstream trend, which relied on pure and straightforward product pushing. With advertising messages centred on family issues, life-work balance and general concerns, Banco Mello managed to capture a significant market share in a short time, in a stagnant mature market that was the banking sector

Royco Cup-a-Soup

Portuguese people are great soup consumers. Cooked with vegetables, noodles, rice, beans, chickpeas, sprouts and sometimes including meat or fish in its preparation, soup is an indispensible first course at every Portuguese table. In a bowl or in a soup dish, and with a spoon. With such an instituted habit, how would a lyophilized 'just-add-water-and-drink-from-a-mug' kind of soup succeed in making its debut? For Royco Cup-a-Soup, the challenge consisted in changing the habits of Portuguese consumers by inducing them to purchase and become regular users of the instant soup. Contrary to regular soup, taken only at mealtimes, Royco Cup-a-Soup could be savoured anywhere, at any time of the day.

A break with current tradition? Yes, but not an impossible mission. In 1997, Royco Cup-a-Soup manufacturer and distributer Fima produced an advertising piece, an innovative and bold film to be shown in television and get consumers to change attitudes. Cleverly positioned as a 'snack', Royco Cup-a-Soup was warm, clever, quirky and trendy, and consumers started to become curious. From then to experimenting was just a small step. The successful advertising film was awarded the "1997 *Grande Prémio RTC*", an award that distinguishes effectiveness and creativity in advertising.

WC Pato

WC Pato was an innovation in the category *Household & body care*. A thick, perfumed detergent inside a plastic bottle with a s-shaped neck, reminding that of a swan, WC Pato's clever packaging managed to reach the inside of toilet bowl rims with ease. With a slogan of "It goes where others cannot" and an advertisement showing a housewife cleaning the toilet bowl without the need of rubber gloves and with a smile upon her lips, WC Pato was a true success in sales.

Mimosa

"Mimosa. A world of trust". This slogan has successfully been used by Mimosa, a Portuguese dairy products brand, which is currently the market leader in the category. Starting by selling milk in cartons, the company soon recognized the need for expansion and decided to embark in a line extension and diversification strategy, in an attempt to grow its market share. The logo was the first change. From red to a stylized sky-blue oval, with touches of prairie-green strokes and using a white non-serifed font reading Mimosa, the new 1990 logo conveyed an image of freshness and confidence. Appearing constantly in TV spots and sponsoring the talk show "A Visita da Cornélia" (Cornélia was a cartoon cow, which gave the

name to the show) the brand rapidly grew in awareness amongst Portuguese audiences. The use of Herman José, the most popular comedian at the time, to voice-over the ads, conferred added value to the brand as people immediately associated him to the brand, and even during his high-rating talk-shows, the identification of his image with such brand was indelible, promoting brand awareness and recall, conveying quality and healthy disposition to the products. Albeit more expensive than competitors, Mimosa milk was a success in sales.

Appealing to people's emotions, it managed to address consumer's hearts, in an intangible path to gain more adepts. This repositioning strategy together with the concerted media campaign granted Mimosa credibility, trust, and a sense of quality among consumers, willing to pay more for what they considered to be a premium product. According to Lactogal's President, Casimiro de Almeida, "people are happy to pay the difference - health is simply priceless".

Renova

Renova enacted a repositioning strategy supported by extensive market research, which pointed out the opportunity of launching new-to-the-market products following an umbrella strategy. Manufacturers of toilet paper, paper napkins and kitchen rolls as well as paper tablecloths, the brand began exploring the use of scents on their products. Supported by scientific research, the brand managed to create new textures, smells and colours to be used by their products. The advertising campaigns that highlighted the tactile, olfactive and visual emotions coming from the use of Renova paper, which was perfectly understood by the market, allowed the company to experience an increase in sales.

Sumol Néctar

Sumol Néctar's début TV with the *"Engarrafamento"* ad (Portuguese term for traffic jam) was bold and irreverent, as it targeted "young adults, with ages ranging from 25 to 35, urban and coming from high and medium-high social classes", as expressed by Refrigor's spokesperson Fernando Tomázio. The company had decided to launch a new to the market high-fruit content (over 50%) juice and hoped it would be welcomed by consumers.

The Portuguese juice and soda market was mature and stagnant at the time. Market studies performed by Marktest indicated that fruit-flavoured sodas were preferred by low-medium income consumers (class c2), aged between 15 to 17, closely followed by those aged between 18 and 24. Predated by cola-flavoured beverages, which held a 35% share, fruit-flavoured juices needed to be constantly innovating in terms of products, and communication with consumers, to keep sales up and maintain their 24% quota in the beverage market. How then, would it be possible for Sumol to grow? The answer was innovation. With the launch of Sumol Néctar, the company targeted older audiences – adults in their prime - with health & wellness concerns, who did not always favour beer or sodas and were not awed by water.

A thick, sweet, flavour-full drink, Sumol Néctar could be enjoyed at breakfast, substituting the morning fruit portion, during a meal, as a healthy alternative to alcoholic beverages and gaseous drinks or during the afternoon or simply as a refreshment beverage; and campaigns told consumers just that - "Do not loose your irreverence, try this healthy alternative".

Super Bock Beer

Amongst the several factors that have contributed to the success of the brand throughout its many years of existence, are the product's – beer – quality, its flavour adaptation to Portuguese palates, the wide distribution network and a solid & coherent communication strategy, with growing investment and sales results.

The market was being literally flooded with new beer brands, but Portuguese beverage manufacturer and distributor Unicer was on its toes. Instead of letting its beer brand Super Bock grow old and unfashionable, the company defined a bold and cautiously planned brand activation strategy, with renewed values and positioning to attract younger and new consumers, retain existing clientele and keep the brand as fashionable and trendy as it had been. The brand's new advertising campaigns constituted a major shift from its previous ones, institutional, built on tradition.

Aggressive and dynamic, the new ads were daring, hip, filled with humour which excited the younger masses whilst delighting older consumers, regular drinkers pleased to watch their favourite beer brand be brought back in style. Not only had they penetrated a new segment, but also had they grown their existing one.

Vespa

By the end of WWII, the brothers Piaggio came up with an economic motorized vehicle, one easy enough to drive and affordable to all Italians: the Vespa motorbike. A symbol of independence and freedom in post-fascist Italy, the product had been conceived with a low cost perspective, in an effort to capture a good market share.

The name Vespa came naturally to Enrico Diageo, arising from the first thought that came to his mind upon looking at the first finished prototype; with a central broad structure designed to best support the driver, and a thin narrow 'waist', idealized for cost and aesthetic purposes, it immediately reminded Enrick of a wasp (in Italian, *vespa*), who exclaimed, "*Mi sembra una*

Vespa!". On April 23rd 1946, Piaggio & C. deposited the patent for a "motorbike with a rational set of organs and elements with chassis in a metal casing covering all mechanic parts". Advertising billboards depicted youngsters in love and happy families with slogans such as *"Vespa: paradiso per due"* ("Vespa, paradise for two") and *"maybe your second car shouldn't be a car"*, thus promoting a product that brought together people from around the world, giving them a reason to cry, laugh, dream and yearn in real life, in books and in the movies.

CHAPTER 15

MODERN ADVERTISING
AND THE NEW CONSUMER

The end of the 20th century had reserved a number of surprises, both in terms of audio track & visual image acquisition and processing as well as in what regarded broadcasting technology. An improved quality in terms of image brings forth a new set of demands, at various levels: planning, direction, and production.

In 1993, Spanish TV network TVE began experimenting with interactive television. The system used resorted to a microcomputer, a screen, a printer, a decoding device and a modem. It required connections to the TV set and to the cable telephone line; users to pay a monthly fee in order to have access to the reduced programgrid that was being aired. Registered viewers were able to participate in live game shows, print recipes that were being featured in culinary programmes and participate in contests for both live shows and interactive advertising spots created specially for this medium.

Japanese multinational Pioneer, widely recognized as an important player in the household electronics market, began shifting its business strategy to include areas with large growth potential, investing on digital audio and video broadcasting systems. The company has also been developing pioneering efforts in the development of pilot solutions for interactive TV, having, among many other initiatives, joined forces with French TV channel "Canal+" to provide the necessary hardware and technical knowledge to deliver digital broadcasts for both regular and interactive TV in France.

Throughout the world, other companies are treading similar paths, with joint ventures being set-up between IT & Electronics corporations and Media & Telecommunication partners, with special incidence on cable networks. This type of co-joint efforts is of the greatest importance, to combine innovation and technology and in the search for new ways to reach audiences with the improved quality and big impact. A solution currently under implementation lies on fibre optics transmissions directed at domestic and corporate customers. Also under optimization are wireless communications and data compression. Upon massification of such technology, borders will be pushed, obstacles overcome and limits be brought to other levels, with numerous possibilities and strategies to deliver new products – and old products in new ways – and explore new business opportunities, together with new target segments.

The use of *video-on-demand* has allowed households to transform their TV sets into truly interactive cinema screens. In the same 'magic box', families have available a computer, a TV set, a telephone, a videophone central and a theatre system. The platform provides access to movies, documentaries, educational & information libraries with millions of entries, carefully organized by whatever order the user chooses – all available at a click on the remote.

To Bill Gates, the key to capitalism is closing the gap between buyers and sellers, an effort that is hopeless without customizable information available. With the internet, buyers and sellers will easily be able to meet without the need for intermediaries. Common sense dictates that to contact a person it is best to opt for sending an email or making a telephone call; when trying to reach millions of people, it may be best to use the television or the printed press. But when the target is made up of a few thousands of individuals, the cost to trace and reach every single one can be a daunting challenge. In the electronic world, this limitation does not exist.

To Jack Nilles (1998), a strong advocate of the ex-office workplace and the father of remote work, it is pointless for workers to waste precious time in heading to and from the office, when they can perform the same tasks sitting in front of a computer or by the telephone, elsewhere. In the early 70s, the author came forward with the concept of *telecommuting*, at a time when the primordial idea lied on establishing satellite offices close to the homes of a significant number of employees in order to save time and increase productivity.

The advent of computers corroborated Niles' thoughts and made his concept a reality. Today, many variations of telecommuting are found in office-home combinations, client's office arrangements and other solutions, not requiring the physical presence of employees for the tasks to be performed in time and with merit.

According to Nilles (1998), in 2017 an estimated 250 million people will opt for developing their work remotely, outside the workplace, 115 million of which in OECD member countries. In Portugal (1999), it was estimated that around 100,000 individuals prefered remote workplaces, constituting 10% of the total workforce dealing with information management.

Frank Feather, a Canadian guru in strategic management consultancy, has also foreseen that, with the advent of electronics, there would be no need for employees to be physically present in their workplace; work would begin as soon as the computer would be turned on. Children would not have the need to go to school, or housewives shopping, as both school and grocery store would come to them via the computer. A trip to the bank would also be a waste of time, as one would be able to fit the bank inside one's pocket and move around with it. Commercial and social transactions would be completely centred on the individual instead of taking place at any given store.

This author was not concerned with the change in paradigm of social relationships. According to his opinion, the technological advances supported by machines and electronic equipment, witnessed in the past decades, have largely and dangerously de-humanized men who ceased to have personal lives the moment they decided to take their work home. Without a clear line separating job and family, both would become entwined and, ultimately, it is the family that will loose. Feather defends that any technological advance should always allow a bipolarized society, dwelling between home and the local community.

Social and economical drivers have contributed to the expansion of telecommuting, among these, the following bear significant importance:

Changes in the workforce: The information management sector, primarily concerned with the creation, manipulation and transmission of information, is the primary US employer, with 60% of the country's workforce dedicated to it. In Europe, although percentages vary from country to country, this is also the sector employing the majority of workers.

Technological development: According to Moore's Law, the cost for processing information drops circa 30% every year. Consequently, many processes can be executed more rapidly and at lower costs. As telecommunication technologies allow for global transmission of increasing packets of information at decreasing costs, this, together with the proliferation of personal computers, should increase the incidence of remote workers. In the nineties over one-third of American homes possessed a PC and the access to the internet has been reporting annual growth rates of around 1500% for the past few years.

Economic and competitive pressures: The rapid expansion of information economy together with the explosion of world demographics has pushed companies into extremely competitive settings. But competition is no longer restricted to finding new customers or keeping old ones; instead, there is an increasing fight for qualified human resources with new skills and education - and it works both ways: if an employee is not satisfied with his current job, he or she can always look for another position with another local / international company.

Traffic and environmental damages: Traffic jams are a side effect of the industrial revolution which held the idea of a centralized workplace close to its heart, thus forcing employees to travel from their homes to the workplace and back every single day. With the number of cars being sold every year rising, as families try to regain control over their lives and use the car to get to and from work, traffic will only get worse... probably everywhere.

CHAPTER 16

COMMUNICATING
IN THE DIGITAL AGE

Throughout the centuries, the major evolutions in terms of communication have been set in motion by the emitter who conveyed the message. With the arrival of the Internet, digital TV and multimedia, the receiver is able, for the first time, to stand in equal terms.

When the first communication intermediaries – books, printed information and so forth - were introduced, the dialogue between emitter and receiver began to cease with the former gaining power over the latter. The media possessed a massifyng and univocal status, with communication flowing in a seemingly downward path, from from priest to the follower, from the ruler to the subject. As rich and poor countries were chronically unbalanced, so were emitters (few and powerful), and receivers (many and powerless).

Monarchies gave way to representative democracies

and with the aid of marketing, it is the consumer (receiver) who determines manufacturing and distribution volumes. At the dawn of the 21st century we are witnessing a change in paradigm, a shift towards a new galaxy of knowledge, attitudes and behaviours - the rising of a new order. This new order, brought forth by the hands of the receiver, is one which will undoubtedly be referred to, by historians, as *"the gates galaxy"*, for the ability it provides to open new doors to communication, for the opportunities it presents to those willing to embrace new & bold changes and unique pathways at a global level, with emitter and receiver equally well-positioned to influence the emerging new digital media, both with similar strength and power.

Emitter and receiver are now able to meet in dialogue, as media can be operated, constrained and released by both.

With the disappearance of communication asymmetries between parties – which was prevalent during the times where radio and TV dominated the media scene – interactivity becomes the rule of thumb. As a consequence, the model known today as mass communication will tendencially decline in favour of massified peer-to-peer operations. To Lester Wunderman, in a near future, companies will not entail conversations with anonymous masses of consumers, but instead with highly individualized targets, capable of formulating their own demands and requirements.

The late nineties

Computers are a reality that can no longer be ignored. Nowadays we are witnessing a true IT explosion at a point where a global peer-to-peer media are in place and used by millions. Following the accelerated shortening of distances brought by the development of faster and more reliable transports, we now see the connection of individuals, at a planetary scale, with efficient, reliable and fast communication tools.

In this digital revolution, information – in its various forms and sizes, from text to voice, from data to image, still or in motion can be accumulated, relayed, transformed and modified in ways up to now unimaginable – and this is influencing organizations, processes, procedures, services, products, jobs and lifestyles.

People today want to be informed and to stay informed. They yearn for receiving more messages than those able to be assimilated. There are systems today that allow for the transfer of information in mere fractions of a second, in volumes that would take an individual many years to do it in the previous century.

Biological pressures (impulse overload), industrial pressure (excess of TV channels) as well as ethical pressures (poor quality of information or deliberately altered information) have shaped individuals into becoming what behavioural scientists and psychologists refer to as "*media prisoners*". Exactly forty years after Marshall McLuhan coined the expression "*global village*", this comes to existence in a spontaneous and unexpected manner, with internet showing that there is a place – a dimension - in society for anarchy to exists, without binding borders or limits.

In this chaotic global network where the main tendency is for people to express themselves and communicate via text messages, it appears that the dominant current of thought has shifted from art to the borders of technology. In fact, with the various formats and amounts of information made available, it is imperative that people possess a highly critical attitude towards what is presented as fact.

Alan C. Kay, an IT expert, wrote: "With the overwhelming increase of available information, much of which untruthful and contradictory, it is imperative that individuals have the ability to discern reality from fiction, to judge the value and validity of what is being conveyed".

The latest concept in these emerging New Media is virtual reality, allowing the user to create and dwell in his unique world of pure imagery, sound and touch, using a computer program with the aid of special equipment including custom-made goggles and gloves.

The information society is an enormous cultural and social challenge, in which all of us – individuals, corporations and institutions – must face with the utmost commitment and dedication. As the Greek philosopher Heraclitus wisely put it "There is nothing more permanent than change".
The emergence of new technologies and the use of the internet will most certainly revolutionize the concept of global communication strategies in the 21st century where the consumer has available, at a click of the mouse, a range of a growing number of fully customizable offerings.

The future of media

Radio: The next big thing for Radio will be interactivity, with shows delivering higher levels of interactivity with listeners, choosing and customizing broadcasts line-ups at their will and according to their preferences. This will constitute a challenge for generalist radios, which currently target masses of anonymous consumers. Audiences will probably not be satisfied to listen to what they do not seek. In the words of radio expert Sena Santos, "radios will have to serve *à la Carte*".

Radio equipments should also suffer alterations, as it is unlikely that people will prefer to have devices exclusively dedicated to transmit radio, when these features can easily be incorporated into TV sets or computer integrated systems. Moreover, with competitors such as digital TV, "Pay TV" and the internet, users are able to select which tunes they want to hear and store them in digital & mobile formats – this is causing a complete paradigm shift for this medium.

Press: As the number of online news editions grow, the sales of paper editions decrease. As media expert Vitor Malheiros stated, "digital will probably overthrow paper". It must not be forgotten that the press is in the information business and not in the paper business, so although the support may change – with the predicted demise of the latter – the business will remain strong, if adapted and adjusted to these new trends.

Multimedia: Multimedia is the present and future for the promotion of brands, as well as for communicating with younger segments. In this digital age, multimedia will be the chosen support available to users who value interactivity, mobility and freedom.

Television: The challenge brought forth by the digital age has caused an increase in the number of available channels and allowed users to perform other tasks using the TV set, such as shopping, gambling, going to the bank, buying tickets for shows and events and surfing the web. British former ministry for science and technology, Ian Taylor, believes that viewers will have full control over channel selection as well as over programming grids and line-ups, chosen according to their preferences. Pay TV gives viewers that chance. Users of Pay TV will only pay for the channels considered to be of interest to them, and are able to select the order in which programmes are shown, which can constitute both an enormous opportunity and an important threat to network management, in which all control is relinquished to evermore specialized and demanding users.

Internet: Internet is undoubtedly one of the key responsible media for the rapid transformations in the overall media industry. Its fast spread and rapid technological development made it possible for this medium to reach the milestone of 10 million users in only five years, a feat when compared to other media, such as the telephone (38 years), the fax (22 years), mobile phones (9 years) and personal computers (7 years). The number of available websites has also been growing at vertiginous levels: between January 1991 and January 1996 it has increased from 500 thousand to an amazing 9.5 million.

Despite these astounding advances, the reality is that we are still at an early stage of sectoral development; only when the computer and TV screens become one will information highways become truly impressive.

Communications, corporate operations, radio and TV broadcasts, educational spaces and commercial transactions will be soon combined into single platforms like the real interactive TV, with emitter and receiver equally positioned to communicate as peers. News will come in at any hour, from anywhere around the planet, and the internet will spread a new universal language, within a globally integrated communication framework.

CHAPTER 17

FINAL CONSIDERATIONS

We all make mistakes, but advertisers cannot afford to err as much as the common person, as his actions will have impact over brands, products, services, companies, and ultimately, on the global economy with an ensuing impact on the social layer.

With growing concerns over the manner in which advertising budgets are put to (good) use and with the emerging technologies available for marketing products and services, advertising agencies will become increasingly scrutinized and pushed towards obtaining tangible and measurable results from their advertising campaigns. In this framework, the knowledge of the market and consumers, as well as the ability to anticipate trends and tendencies, will become as precious an asset as creativity, with some advertising agencies already investing in research centres and observatories focused on taking the pulse of society and respective evolution pathways. Amongst the many variables, a few stand out for their relevance and importance. Such is the case of:

Demographic trends: Society has become evermore individualistic. The number of single people is growing fast, composed by single individuals, such as young singles, divorcees and widowers. Youth has become an extended life stage, not only due to the increase in expected lifespan but also because of social issues which tend to push young adults into leaving their parents' home at a more advanced age, for reasons of career development or the formation of family nuclei, happening later in life. According to an article appearing in French magazine *Le Capital*, around 50% of Parisians are currently unmarried youngsters, divorced or widowers, a demographic trend that may become more noticable in the upcoming years.

Society's individual characteristics are also reflected in the usage of the Internet as a privileged means for promoting products and services. As the web becomes an evermore popular meeting place for – not only but also – singles and celibatarians, it becomes a unique media to convey advertising messages targeting these audiences, with experts considering the web as a key meduim for many small businesses

Ecology and Health: Green is good. Bio, light, vitamins

and natural is good! Such are today's buzzwords in a planet where health benefits are valued and viewed as benefits impossible to forego.

The concern with cardiac diseases associated with high cholesterol levels and with aesthetics (in which obesity is the main enemy, especially for female audiences) has opened up a space for the emergence of a new market segment, in which low-fat & reduced calories products are truly best-sellers.

Moral and Ethics: Delivering truthful messages will become an imperative for both companies and advertisers, as consumers have access to information and the opportunity for product comparison. Ethics and credibility are now the new benchmarks in advertising, critical to the effectiveness of promotional campaigns and to the ensuing success of brands, products and services. Flooded by numerous messages, consumers will tend to become insensitive to meaningless and shallow campaigns, valuing creativity, idoneity, truthfulness and benefits derived there from. Whilst creativity is a competence of advertising agencies, idoneity, truthfulness and initiative are of the responsibility of the manufacturers and distributers engaging advertisers to promote their offerings, which need to create and implement a series of mechanisms aiming at capturing audiences' trust. A simple example is that of a bank promising to perform a certain banking operation in a certain number of days; if the deadline is exceeded, the bank must, at all costs, apologise to the customer and offer some alternate form of compensation.

Consumers are no longer contented with vague promises, but are thirsty for value propositions, built on truth and commitment and expect companies and advertisers to ensure that this will occur. Companies must, therefore and at all times, commit to the messages conveyed in their promotional campaigns whilst making every possible endeavour to supply reliable and trustworthy information to its stakeholders.

Dreams and the Return of *Glamour*: The hardships brought about by current social and economic contexts, with particular relevance for the growing concerns towards unemployment, have redefined the concept of dreams. Whilst the eighties fostered the export of unlimited consumption from the US to European territories, the nineties witnessed a decrease in available income which enabled advertisers to explore dream-like scenarios, providing audiences the opportunity to escape, even if momentarily, from their troubles, fears and anxieties.

With consumers being evermore cautious with respect to the amounts they spend, it is necessary that companies offer products with added value and with intangible benefits on top of tangible characteristics.

Dream, evasion and *glamour* are what the *apport* top models bring to today's advertising. Whilst in the eighties engaging a model to advertise a product was regarded as poor creativity, in the nineties, these rules have changed. Today's recession concerns, allied to the growing uncertainty of an economic *reprise*, reduces the propensity for both companies and advertisers to take risks – even if calculated ones. As a result, top models have experienced a growth in demand for their appearance in promotional pieces, for the certainty of return it provides to the investment, more so, when considering the increased appetence for dream, evasion and glamour demanded by consumers and fulfilled by the inclusion of beautiful men and women in advertisements.

The Senior Market: Albeit directly related to demographic trends, the senior target deserves undivided attention from advertisers. European and US population is ageing at a never before witnessed pace. Nowadays, a man or a woman in his/her sixties can no longer be referred to as being old, especially if living in large cities. "Sixties is the new forties", as experts put it; in fact, a sixty year-old person is intellectually and physically fit and actively employed or performing value-adding activities. The opportunities for offering new products and/or services to this segment is enormous; from health to food and nutrition, from leisurely activities to luxury products, there are many categories and niches still waiting to be explored. Adding all this to the fact that the elderly segment usually spends a larger amount of time watching TV – the preferred vehicle for advertising to this segment – it is easily understandable that this age group will be an indentified target for corporations in the very near future.

Male vs. Feminine Values: To Jacques Seguella, male values will be progressively replaced by feminine values; in this manner, attributes such as strength, courage and attitude, typically associated to industrialism, war and violence, will gradually be replaced by others pertaining to balance, harmony and tolerance. This progressive prevalence of feminine values finds echo in the increased offering of products and services to female audiences, a target growing in visibility and importance.

Philip Kotler, in his book *"Rethinking the Future"*, expressed his views on future advertising trends, based on his experience as a marketer and businessman, which relied on nine pillars:

Explosion of Entertainment: The modern consumer will seek entertainment, either at work or at home, whether whilst shopping or when working out at the gym. Time is scarce, and this forces people to perform several tasks at once. Retailers have already identified this trend, providing true shopping experiences to customers.

Nike stores are a good example, with customers walking trough water tanks filled with fish, stepping on TV screens playing the latest hit songs, while contemplating sports memorabilia. They can try out a new pair of sneakers and, at the same time, shoot hoops. In the same manner, museums and concert halls will cease to simply display their collections and works of art, turning them into integrated multimedia centres for entertainment experiences.

High-Yield Consumers: The middle class will no longer be the reference for target segmentation; there will be A-type segments and C-type targets. The offering for the former will be high quality premium products and personalized services at premium prices, whilst the offerings for the latter should be based on money-saving paradigms.

The Importance of Brands: A customer will always tend to compare brands. Distributors have opted for selling own brand products at lower prices, but with quality, key characteristics and, more importantly, with a packaging that is very similar to branded products – these can be placed side-by side to foster price comparison and push customers into choosing the most cost-efficient alternative – their white-labeled brand instead of purchasing the branded alternative. Also, own brand products are made similar to the market leader or the second best in each category, since, with the abundance of goods and brands, the consumer is only able to retain but a few names from those products that sell the most.

Quality vs. Price vs. Service: The key is to sell high quality – real or perceived – for a little less than competitors. Service will become a differentiation factor, allowing for a more complete and valuable offering.

Causal Marketing: Sponsoring environmental causes, like Body Shop does, conveys a notion of social and environmental responsibility to consumers, transporting the brand beyond the mere product and associating it with higher values and causes. Coca-Cola addresses the *"human family"*, while Reebok claims *"this is my planet"*. This creates indelible links between causes, purposes and products, fostering an osmosis of values that motivates the act of purchase.

Product Differentiation: Differentiation is a strategy aiming at standing out from equals. An efficient implementation makes use of the marketing mix's four *P's*: product, promotion, price and point of sale.

Enhancement of the *Loyalty Effect*: Retaining customers and managing to keep them loyal to a brand, product or service is, in principle, easier than capturing and retaining new customers. The *Loyalty Effect* was first introduced by Frederick Reicheld, loyalty director at Bain.

Interactive Marketing: Contrary to standard marketing

models - criticized for being too deterministic, while considering customers as being merely passive recipients - interactive marketing encourages both parties, buyers and sellers, to be engaged in the decision-making process, which will bemore successful as both sides exhibit higher competences and skills.

One to One Marketing: One to one marketing is the epitome of personalized interaction with the customer. Pioneered by Don Peppers and Martha Rogers, the model regards each consumer as unique and seeks to discover his needs before putting forward a value proposition.

The gradual disappearance of generalist TV channels and the increase of specific, niche-targeting broadcasts will soon be a reality with growing expression.

In the following years, the current *push* strategy observed in sales will be progressively replaced by offering the customer what he or she really needs.

Massified targets will revert to distinguishable, unique individuals or group of individuals also called *tribes*; general contents will be replaced by tailor-made solutions; distances will be shortened, people will be brought together, interacting with one another in a concerted effort to create value.

...

THE END

SUGGESTED READINGS

Books

Brochand, B., Lendrevie, J., Rodrigues, J. D. & Dionísio, P. (1999). Publicitor. Publicações Dom Quixote, Lisboa, Portugal, 654 pp.

Coelho, P. (1998). Veronica decide morrer. Editora Objectiva, Ltda., Rio de Janeiro, Brazil, 242 pp.

Davis, W. & McCormack, A. (1979). The Information Age. Addison Wesley Longman Publishing Co., Massachusetts, USA, 427 pp.

Samuelson, P. A. & Nordhaus, W. D. (1992). Economics. McGraw-Hill, 14th ed., London, UK, 908 pp.
Joannis, H. (1988). Le processus de création publicitaire. Bordas, Paris, France, 177 pp.

Klapp, O. E.(1986). Overload and Boredom: Essays on the Quality of Life in the Information Society (Contributions in Sociology). Greenwood Pub Group, USA, 192 pp.

Kotler, P. (1998). Rethinking Markets, Mapping the Future Marketplace, In: Rethinking the Future: Rethinking Business, Principles, Competition, Control & Complexity, Leadership, Markets, and the World. R. Gibson (Ed.) Nicholas Brealey Publishing, Boston, USA, pp. 196-210.

Kotler, P. & Amstrong, G. (1998). Principles of Marketing. Prentice Hall College Div., 8th ed.,720 pp.

Martins, I. N. & Carvalho, T. D. (1990). Psicologia - Ser e Conhecer. Texto Editora Lda, Lisbon, Portugal, 231 pp.

Nilles, J. M. (1998). Managing Telework: Options for Managing the Virtual Workforce, John Wiley & Sons, Inc., New York, USA, 352 pp.

Rapp, S. & Collins, T. (1995). The New Maxi Marketing McGraw Hill, New York, USA, 352 pp.

Ries, A. (1996). Focus, The Future of Your Company Depends on It. Harper Collins Publishers, New York, USA, 304 pp.

Trout, J. (1996). The New Positioning. McGraw Hill, London, UK, 1st ed., 173 pp.

Wiersema, F. (1998). Customer Intimacy. Knowledge

Exchange, 1st ed., 221pp.

Wunderman, L. (1996). Being Direct, Making Advertising Pay. Random House Publisher, 1st ed., New York, USA , 336pp.

Resesarch papers and studies

"Brand asset valuator" by Young & Rubicam, 1996.

"O percurso do consumidor português", by Nova Publicidade, 1997.

"Hábitos e atitudes dos consumidores perante os meios de comunicação", by J. W. Thompson, 1997.

"Impacto dos blocos publicitários em televisão", by Plurimarketing, 1998 .

Publications and articles

Almeida, A. (1996). Super Bock, uma linguagem para a cerveja. Briefing 170, 10.

Araújo, B. (1996). Marcas de mãos dadas. Exame 97, 76.

Araújo, B., Vasco, R., Costa, A. e Miranda, M. (1997).

Dossier casos de sucesso em Portugal. Exame Marketing 100 (1), 29 - 82.

Baltazar, T. (1997). Estrangeirismos. Briefing 176, 32.

Baptista, C. (1999). Discussão nos bastidores. Suplemento Marketing & Publicidade do Diário de Notícias, 6 – 8.

Belo, J. (1997). Nizan Guanaes. Briefing 185, 12 – 13.

Bernardo, N. (1997). Vender na internet. Fortuna 63, 94 – 96.

Bernardo, N. (1997). Medir audiências. Fortuna 67, 88 – 90.

Bernardo, N. (1998). Páginas na internet. Fortuna 71, 52 – 53.

Blecher, N. (1997). A magia da publicidade invisível. Executive Digest, 120 – 124.

Brito, P. (1999). A futura geração Y. Suplemento Marketing & Publicidade do Diário de Notícias, 36 – 37

Brody, J. (1997). Anda a dormir o suficiente? Selecções do Readers Digest, 43 – 47.

Cabral, F. S. (1997). Os custos da globalização. Fortuna 66, 42 – 43.

Camacho, J. (1999). Daciano Costa. Page 9, 12 – 17.

Campos, J. (1996). A Fast pub. Briefing 170, 28.

Canha, I. (1997). O elogio do teletrabalho. Executive Digest, 86 – 87.

Cardoso, P. (1999). Como um bisturi. Suplemento Marketing & Publicidade do Diário de Notícias, 24 – 25.

Carvalho, I. (1998). Televisão a três dimensões. Fortuna 71, 120.

Correia, G. (1997). Os mercados do futuro. Exame Marketing 100 (1), 8 – 11.

Correia, G. (1997). Publicidade na net. Exame 105, 114 – 117.

Costa, A. (1997). Mau olhado. Quo 25, 30 – 35.

Cruz, L. (1996). O futuro da internet. Fortuna 55, 96.
Dhombres, D., Pomonti, J., Maringues, M. e Philip, B. (1997). Cidades do excesso. Selecções do Readers Digest, 56 – 61.

Eleutério, V. (1999). Da publicidade que foi. Suplemento Marketing & Publicidade do Diário de Notícias, 48 – 50.

F., S. F. (1997). Portugal social em números. Fortuna 58, 135.

Faria, H. (1996). Alinhamentos internacionais. Fortuna 56, 96 – 98.

Faria, H. (1997). Anunciantes regressam às salas de cinema. Fortuna 59, 18.

Faria, H. (1997). Direct mail. Fortuna 61, 90 – 92.

Ferreira, A. (1999). Ousar e reinventar. Suplemento Marketing & Publicidade do Diário de Notícias, 46.

Galvin, V. (1995). Ruído por favor. Quo 3, 34 – 37.

Garcez, P. (1997). Tocando os limites. Ingénium 21, 78 – 79.

Gomes, F. (1997). Caça anúncios. Fortuna 61, 106.

Gomes, F. (1999). Profecias e conceitos de personagens futuristas no tempo presente. Page 9, 10 – 11.

Gomes, Y. (1997). Parto-me a rir. Quo 25, 18 – 24.

Gomes, Y. (1997). Web side story. Quo 25, 82 – 87

Guedes, J. (1995). Esta empresa é uma ruína. Quo 3, 80 – 83.

L, J. (1994). Criatividade em toda a linha. Marketing e publicidade 71, 36 – 38.

Lenzner, R. (1997). O mundo visto por Peter Druker. Executive Digest, 90 – 98.

Machado, R. (1999). Quanto custa a verdade. Suplemento Marketing & Publicidade do Diário de Notícias, 16 – 19.

Magalhães, C. (1997). AGB vai medir share da Tv Cabo. Briefing 178, 6.

Magalhães, C. (1997). Agência - Cliente: amigos para sempre? Briefing 179, 19.

Magalhães, C. (1997). Perfil do utilizador da internet. Briefing 180, 14.
Magalhães, C. (1997). Estudos de mercado. Briefing 180, 25 – 30.

Magalhães, C. (1997). O pequeno consumidor em Portugal. Briefing 185, 4.

Magalhães, C. (1997). Dossier televisão. Briefing 186, 21 – 26.

Magalhães, C. (1997). A televisão sempre. Briefing 187, 12.

Magalhães, C. (1997). Produtoras de imagem e de som. Briefing 187, 21 – 26.

Magalhães, C. (1997). A revolução Luso - Brasileira. Briefing 188, 6 – 7.

Magalhães, C. (1997). Cannes 1997. Briefing 190, 17 – 30.

Martins, R. (1994). Reebok cria equipa de sonho. Marketing e Publicidade 71, 44.

Matos, M. (1999). Grafitti. Page 9, 40 – 45.

Mello, A. (1999). Vale tudo menos proibir. Suplemento Marketing & Publicidade do Diário de Notícias, 30.

N., C., D. (1997). A arma da comparação. Fortuna 68, 38.

Neves, C. (1997). Anunciar na televisão. Fortuna 62, 92 – 96.

Neves, C. (1997). Entre na internet. Fortuna 63, 104.

Neves, C. (1997). Patrocínio e mecenato. Fortuna 84 – 88.

Nogueira, A. (1997). Como se fabrica um êxito de bilheteira. Marketeer 11, 36 – 41.

Patarrana, M. (1999). Os quês no século. Suplemento Marketing & Publicidade do Diário de Notícias, 38 – 39.

Ramos, S. (1996). Jovens contra a corrente. Fortuna 52, 100.

Ramos, S. (1997). Marcas globais. Fortuna 67, 92 – 96.

Ramos, S. (1997). Relações com qualidade. Fortuna 69, 86 – 87.

Ribeiro, L. (1997). O mundo na era virtual. Executive Digest, 62 – 70.

Ribeiro, L. (1997). Quem tem medo do camaleão. Marketeer 11, 1.

Rodrigues, L. (1999). Navegar no futuro. Suplemento Marketing & Publicidade do Diário de Notícias, 42 – 43.

Rosário, A. (1999). Classificados. Suplemento Marketing & Publicidade do Diário de Notícias, 14 – 15.

Saavedra, R. (1999). O elogio da traça. Suplemento Marketing & Publicidade do Diário de Notícias, 3.

Sacadura, J. (1997). Não havia nechechidade. Briefing 188, 25.

Santos, F. (1999). Rasguem as tabelas. Suplemento Marketing & Publicidade do Diário de Notícias, 22.

Santos, J. (1997). Comunicar na era digital. Marketeer 11, 42 – 46.

Sequeira, S. (1997). A publicidade pimba. Briefing 188, 40.

Serpa, M. (1997). A universalidade do visual. Briefing 193, 6.

Silva, C. (1996). Pioneer aposta na televisão do futuro. Exame 97, 36 – 37.

Silva, C. (1997). Hipermania. Exame Marketing 100 (1), 92 – 97.

Silva, M. (1994). Perceber o consumidor. Marketing e Publicidade 71, 48.

Silva, M. (1999). A difícil tarefa. Suplemento Marketing

& Publicidade do Diário de Notícias, 35.

Simões, N. (1996). A televisão do futuro. Briefing 174, 16.

Tavares, I. (1997). Publirevolução. Fortuna 66, 47 – 61.

Trigo, R. (1999). Privilégio às ideias. Suplemento Marketing & Publicidade do Diário de Notícias, 44.

Trindade, B. (1996). A revolução na publicidade. Briefing 175, 9.

Trindade, B. (1997). Agências de publicidade em exame. Briefing 182, 6.

Trindade, B. (1997). A má publicidade é um facto. Briefing 194, 10.

Vasco, R. (1997). Os gestores de quem se fala. Exame Marketing 100 (1), 84 – 90.

Vasco, R. (1997). 6 Grandes tendências para o século XX. Exame Marketing 100 (1), 98 – 101.

Vasco, R. (1997). As campanhas mais admiradas. Exame Marketing 100 (1), 108 – 109.

Vieira, S. (1997). Prisioneiro Mediáticos. Ingénium 98.

Wengoróvius, J. (1999). Só estou bem onde não estou. Suplemento Marketing & Publicidade do Diário de Notícias, 40

Interviews

The author would like to thank the following communication & advertising experts:
Rosalina Machado; Thiago Baltazar; Fernando Correia dos Santos; Pedro Mota Carmo; Luís Reis, Pedro Bidarra.